# The Hidden Books of Creation

*Jewish Mysticism, The Tree of Life, and the Secrets of the Cosmos*

**A Modern Translation**

Adapted for the Contemporary Reader

**Various Ancient Writers**

Translated by Tim Zengerink

# Table of Contents

# Preface - Message to the Reader

**What If You Could Help Rebuild the Greatest Library in Human History?**

Thousands of years ago, the Library of Alexandria stood as the crown jewel of human achievement — a sanctuary where the collected wisdom of every known civilization was gathered, preserved, and shared freely.

And then, it was lost.

Through fire, conquest, and the slow erosion of time, humanity lost not just books — but ideas, dreams, discoveries, and stories that could have changed the world forever.

Today, the Library of Alexandria lives again — and you are invited to be a part of its restoration.

Our mission is simple yet profound:

To rebuild the greatest library the world has ever known, and to translate all timeless works into every language and dialect, so that no seeker of knowledge is ever left behind again.

By joining our movement to rebuild the modern Library of Alexandria, you become part of an unprecedented mission:

- **Unlimited Access to the Greatest Audiobooks & eBooks Ever Written:**

    Instantly explore thousands of legendary works—Plato, Shakespeare, Jane Austen, Leo Tolstoy, and countless more. All instantly available to read or listen, placing a complete literary universe at your fingertips.

- **Beautiful Paperback & Deluxe Editions at Printing Cost**

  Own any title as an elegant paperback, deluxe hardcover, or stunning collectible boxset—offered to you at true printing cost, delivered straight to your door. Build your personal Library of Alexandria, crafted for beauty, built for durability, and worthy of proud display.

- **Fresh Translations for Modern Readers—in Every Language & Dialect**

  Enjoy timeless masterpieces reimagined in clear, contemporary language—no more outdated phrases or obscure references. Alongside the original versions, we're tirelessly translating these classics into every language and dialect imaginable, ensuring accessibility and understanding across cultures and generations.

- **Join a Global Renaissance of Literature & Knowledge**

  You directly support expanding our library, publishing deluxe editions at true cost, translating works into all global languages, and bringing humanity's greatest stories to people everywhere. By joining today, you're not just preserving a legacy of masterpieces; you set in motion a powerful wave of literary accessibility.

**Become a Torchbearer of Knowledge.**

Join us for free now at **LibraryofAlexandria.com**

Together, we will ensure that the light of human wisdom never fades again.

With gratitude and a shared love of knowledge,
The Modern Library of Alexandria Team

Visit:

www.libraryofalexandria.com

Or scan the code below:

# Introduction

## The Mystical Blueprint of the Universe

From the beginning of human thought, there has been an insatiable desire to understand the nature of existence—how the universe came to be, why time unfolds in patterns, and what hidden forces guide the destinies of people and nations. While modern science offers frameworks rooted in mathematics and physics, ancient mystics turned to the divine, unveiling systems that linked creation itself with spiritual truth. Two of the most profound documents born from this tradition are The Book of Jubilees and Sefer Yetzirah, known as The Book of Creation. These texts present not merely histories or metaphysical speculation, but blueprints—sacred maps of how the universe was spoken into being, how time was measured before clocks, and how the forces of life, death, and destiny swirl together in divine symmetry.

The Hidden Books of Creation unites these two deeply mysterious texts into one volume, allowing readers to experience the esoteric wisdom of Jewish mysticism through a modern lens. Each text provides a different yet complementary pathway to understanding creation. Jubilees, often called the "Lesser Genesis," offers a retelling of the biblical narrative infused with cosmic order, calendars, and angelic intervention. Sefer Yetzirah, by contrast, is far more abstract— a cryptic manual on the structure of the cosmos through divine letters, numbers, and elemental forces. Taken together, these writings are not simply intellectual exercises. They are invitations to enter the sacred architecture of the world.

Throughout history, these texts have captivated the minds of rabbis, mystics, philosophers, and seekers. Their language is encoded with symbolism and layered meaning, inviting contemplation and inner transformation. This modern translation offers both clarity and reverence—rendering their insights accessible while preserving their mystical force.

## The Book of Jubilees: Time, Angels, and Sacred History

The Book of Jubilees claims to be a divine revelation given to Moses atop Mount Sinai—an expanded version of Genesis and Exodus delivered not for the masses, but for those ready to understand the spiritual framework behind biblical events. It recounts the history of the world from creation to the giving of the law, structured not by arbitrary chronology but by a sacred calendar of "jubilee" periods—forty-nine-year cycles that reflect divine rhythms of time and history.

In this cosmology, time itself is sacred, a living expression of God's will. The division of weeks, years, and jubilees mirrors the pattern of creation, emphasizing that history is not random but divinely measured. The events of human life—from births and deaths to blessings and judgments—fall within these ordained cycles. The Book of Jubilees insists that to understand time is to understand the hidden order of God.

Angels play a central role in this vision. They are not simply messengers but cosmic agents, charged with recording human deeds, executing divine judgment, and guarding the heavenly structure of time. Jubilees reveals a richly layered spiritual world, where heavenly beings oversee the unfolding of sacred history. The book reinforces the belief that human actions are part of a larger drama—one that is watched, recorded, and ultimately judged by divine powers.

One of the text's most provocative elements is its insistence on predestination and moral clarity. It presents a world sharply divided between good and evil, righteousness and corruption, with the covenant people of Israel called to preserve divine order through obedience to the law. Yet within this strict framework, there is also immense beauty: in the cycles of rest, in the sacredness of the land, in the prophetic anticipation of a messianic age.

Jubilees is a call to see the cosmos not as a machine but as a temple—a sanctuary where time, matter, and morality converge in sacred harmony.

## Sefer Yetzirah:
## Letters, Numbers, and the Tree of Life

If Jubilees is mystical history, Sefer Yetzirah is mystical science. One of the oldest texts of Kabbalistic thought, Sefer Yetzirah (The Book of Creation) outlines a radical vision of the universe's construction. It teaches that God created the world through "32 paths of wisdom"— ten sefirot (divine emanations) and twenty-two Hebrew letters. Together, these elements form the spiritual code of reality: a divine alphabet and numerical framework through which all things were made.

According to Sefer Yetzirah, these letters are not merely symbols; they are living energies. Each one carries a frequency, a function, and a role in the architecture of existence. By combining and permuting these letters, God formed everything—from the stars and planets to the elements of fire, water, and air. The universe is, quite literally, a divine utterance—written in a language of light and form.

The ten sefirot, meanwhile, form the skeletal structure of creation—the Tree of Life. These are not physical objects but metaphysical vessels, channels through which divine energy flows. They represent principles such as wisdom, understanding, strength, beauty, and sovereignty. Together, they map the relationship between the infinite and the finite, the Creator and creation. They also reflect the structure of the human soul, suggesting that the cosmos is mirrored within us.

Sefer Yetzirah also presents a theory of time rooted in cycles of space and matter. The twelve signs of the zodiac, the seven planets, and the three elemental forces are each assigned to letters and paths, suggesting a grand unity between heaven and earth. This cosmology is not meant to be understood mechanically, but meditatively. The text encourages readers to contemplate, pronounce, and even breathe the letters—to align oneself with the vibrations of the divine.

Throughout Jewish mystical history, Sefer Yetzirah has served as both a sacred riddle and a practical guide. It has influenced the development of Kabbalah, inspired numerological systems, and challenged philosophers to think beyond material causation. It is a key that opens the gate to a universe built not of atoms alone, but of spirit, thought, and sacred sound.

## The Unity of Heaven, Earth, and Mind

These two texts—Jubilees and Sefer Yetzirah—seem at first to belong to very different worlds. One is a narrative of history, the other a diagram of metaphysics. But at their core, they both reflect the same fundamental truth: that the universe is not chaotic, but divinely ordered. That time, space, and language are sacred. That the destiny of humanity is interwoven with cosmic rhythms. And that wisdom, once hidden, can be revealed.

Their teachings continue to shape the heart of Jewish mystical thought. They provide the foundation for later works such as the

Zohar, the Bahir, and the mystical commentaries on Torah that proliferated through medieval and modern Kabbalah. They inspire not only theologians, but poets, artists, and scientists—anyone who senses that behind the veil of the visible lies a deeper structure.

This modern translation seeks to honor the complexity and beauty of these ancient texts while making them accessible to contemporary readers. Archaic formulations have been clarified, dense symbolic phrases have been gently opened, and the structure of each work has been preserved to maintain its spiritual rhythm.

Whether you are a seasoned student of Kabbalah, a curious newcomer to Jewish mysticism, or simply a seeker of truth, these books offer not just knowledge, but transformation. They invite you to view creation not as a puzzle to be solved, but as a mystery to be entered.

May the hidden wisdom of these sacred texts illuminate your understanding of the universe and your place within it. May you discover, as the ancients did, that the secret of creation is not just out there—but also within.

# The Book of Jubilees

## Introduction

The Book of Jubilees, also known as "The Little Genesis," is an ancient Jewish text that expands on the stories in Genesis and Exodus. It was likely written between the 2nd and 1st centuries BCE and retells biblical history using a unique system of time—dividing events into periods of forty-nine years, called jubilees. This structure provides a detailed timeline from creation up to the moment when God gave the law at Mount Sinai. The book also gives insight into ancient Jewish beliefs, laws, and traditions.

What makes Jubilees unique is its strong focus on the idea that God's laws came directly from Him, the importance of the Sabbath, and the role of angels in delivering God's messages. The text reflects the beliefs and customs of a particular Jewish group, possibly connected to the Essenes. While it is not included in the Hebrew Bible, it is considered a sacred text in the Ethiopian Orthodox Church and is valued for its deep religious and historical meaning.

This important book acts as a link between the Bible and later writings about the end times, giving us a better understanding of biblical stories and the culture and religious practices of that time.

## Chapter I.

In the first year after the Israelites left Egypt, on the sixteenth day of the third month, God spoke to Moses, saying, "Come up to Me on the mountain, and I will give you two stone tablets with My laws and commandments. You will teach them to the people."

Moses went up Mount Sinai, and God's glory covered the mountain in a cloud for six days. On the seventh day, God called to Moses from the cloud. His presence on the mountaintop looked like a blazing fire. Moses stayed on the mountain for forty days and forty nights, and during this time, God showed him past and future events, organizing all the laws and teachings.

God said, "Pay close attention to everything I am telling you and write it down in a book. In the future, people will realize that even when they sin and break My covenant, I have not abandoned them. When these events take place, they will understand that My judgments are right and fair. They will see that I have always been with them."

Write down everything I tell you today because I already know how stubborn and rebellious they will be. Even before I bring them into the land I promised to their ancestors—Abraham, Isaac, and Jacob—they will turn away from Me. They will enjoy all its blessings, eat until they are full, and then follow false gods that cannot save them when trouble comes. This will stand as a witness against them. They will forget My commandments and follow the sinful ways of the nations around them, worshiping idols and practicing evil. These false gods will become a trap and a burden to them.

Many will die or be taken captive by their enemies because they rejected My laws. They will stop celebrating My holy days, break My Sabbaths, and abandon the sacred place I gave them. Instead, they will build altars on high places, worship idols, and even sacrifice their children to demons. They will do terrible things because of the evil in their hearts.

I will send messengers to warn them, but they will refuse to listen. They will kill these messengers, persecute those who follow My law, and twist My words to justify their wrongdoing. Because of this, I will turn away from them and allow foreign nations to capture them and destroy their land. They will be scattered among different nations, and while in exile, they will forget My laws and commandments. They will lose understanding of My holy days and drift even further from Me.

But one day, they will return to Me with all their heart, soul, and strength. When they truly seek Me, they will find Me. I will bring them back from the nations where they were scattered and give them peace and righteousness. I will fill them with goodness and bless them instead of cursing them. They will no longer be the oppressed but the leaders.

I will place My sanctuary among them and live with them. I will be their God, and they will be My people, walking in truth and righteousness. I will never leave them because I am their Lord and God.

Moses fell on his face and prayed, saying, "O Lord, do not abandon Your people, Your chosen ones. Do not let them fall into the hands of their enemies, who will lead them further into sin. Show them mercy, Lord. Create a pure spirit within them so they do not continue down the path of evil and perish before You. They are Your people, whom You saved with great power from Egypt. Give them clean hearts and holy spirits so they do not fall into sin again."

The Lord answered Moses, "I know how stubborn they are. They will not fully obey Me until they admit their sins and the sins of their ancestors. But when they return to Me with all their heart and soul, I will change them. I will give them new hearts, and their children will follow Me as well. I will fill them with My holy spirit and purify them, so they will never turn away from Me again. They will obey My laws, and I will be their Father, and they will be My children. Everyone in heaven and on earth will know that they are My people, and I am their God. I love them with an everlasting love.

Write down everything I am telling you—past, present, and future.

These words will stand for all generations, guiding them until I come to live among them forever."

Then God said to the angel of His presence, "Write everything down for Moses, from the beginning of creation until the time My sanctuary will be built forever among them." The Lord will reveal Himself to all, and everyone will know that He is the God of Israel, the Father of Jacob's descendants, and the eternal King who reigns from Mount Zion. Jerusalem and Zion will be holy forever.

The angel of the presence, who guided Israel through the wilderness, brought the tablets containing the history of the world—from the creation of time to the final renewal of heaven and earth. All creation will be restored as it was meant to be, and the Lord's sanctuary will be established in Jerusalem on Mount Zion. The stars and heavenly lights will be renewed, bringing healing, peace, and blessings to God's chosen people forever.

# Chapter II.

Then the angel, following God's command, spoke to Moses and said, "Write down the full story of creation. Record how, in six days, God made everything and brought it to life. On the seventh day, He rested and made it a special, holy day for all time.

On the first day, God created the sky, the earth, and the waters. He also made angels—some to be in His presence, some to bring holiness, and others to control fire, wind, clouds, snow, hail, and frost. He created angels for thunder, lightning, and the changing seasons. He also made spirits for all His creatures, both in heaven and on earth. He formed the deep waters, darkness, evening, night, light, dawn, and daytime. Everything was made with His wisdom. We saw His creation and praised Him. Seven great things were made on the first day.

On the second day, God made the sky and placed it between the waters. Some waters rose above the sky, while others remained below, covering the earth. This was the only thing He created on the second day.

On the third day, God commanded the waters under the sky to come together so that dry land would appear. The waters obeyed, forming seas, rivers, and lakes. On this day, He also created dew, seeds, and plants. He made fruit trees, forests, and the Garden of Eden, filled with all kinds of plants. Four important things were made on the third day.

On the fourth day, God made the sun, moon, and stars. He placed them in the sky to shine on the earth, to separate day from night, and to mark time. These lights were also signs for the days, the Sabbath, the months, festivals, years, and special cycles of time. Three great things were made on the fourth day.

On the fifth day, God created the great sea creatures that live in the deep waters. These were the first living things He made. He also created fish and all creatures that live in water, as well as all kinds of birds. When the sun rose, it shone on these creatures and blessed them, along with all the plants and trees that grow on the earth. Three kinds of living beings were made on the fifth day.

On the sixth day, God made land animals, including livestock and creatures that move on the ground. After that, He created humans, making both man and woman. He gave them control over the earth, the seas, the birds, the animals, and all living things. They were put in charge of everything on earth. Four types of creation were made on the sixth day, bringing the total to twenty-two.

On this day, God finished all His work—the heavens, the earth, the seas, and everything in them. He established a special sign: the

Sabbath. He commanded that people should work for six days and rest on the seventh.

God also told His angels to observe the Sabbath with Him, both in heaven and on earth. Then He said, "I will choose a special people from all the nations, and they will keep the Sabbath. I will make them My people and bless them, just as I have blessed and set apart this day for Myself. They will belong to Me, and I will be their God.

From everything I have seen, I have chosen Jacob's descendants as My firstborn son. I have set them apart forever and will teach them to honor the Sabbath, so they may rest and keep it holy."

That is why the Sabbath is a sign—a day to celebrate with food, drink, and praise to the Creator. Just as God chose a special people, they will keep the Sabbath and celebrate with us.

His commandments were given as a way to praise Him forever.

From Adam to Jacob, there were twenty-two generations, just like there were twenty-two kinds of work completed before the seventh day. The Sabbath was blessed along with the days before it, making it a time of holiness and rest.

To Jacob and his descendants, God gave the promise that they would be a holy and blessed people. This was part of His first law and covenant, just as He blessed the Sabbath.

In six days, God created the heavens, the earth, and everything in them. On the seventh day, He made it holy. He commanded that anyone who works on this day must be punished, and anyone who disrespects it will suffer.

Teach the Israelites to keep this day holy and rest from all work, for it is the most sacred of all days. Whoever disrespects it will be punished, and whoever works on it will face consequences forever.

14

This law was given so that the Israelites would always observe the Sabbath and never lose their inheritance. It is a holy and blessed day.

Those who honor it and rest will also be holy and blessed, just as we are.

Tell the Israelites to always keep the Sabbath. Let them know that on this day, they should not do unnecessary work, seek their own pleasure, prepare food or drink, fetch water, or carry heavy loads through their gates. All of this must be done on the sixth day.

They should also not move things between houses on the Sabbath. This day is even more sacred than a jubilee. We in heaven have been observing the Sabbath long before it was given to humans.

The Creator blessed this day, but He did not require every nation to follow it. He set Israel apart to keep this law. Only they were chosen to eat, drink, and celebrate the Sabbath on earth.

The Creator made this day special, setting it apart as the holiest and most honored of all days.

This law was given to the Israelites as a lasting command for all generations.

# Chapter III.

During the second week, over six days, we brought all kinds of animals to Adam. On the first day, he saw wild animals, on the second, livestock, on the third, birds, on the fourth, land creatures, and on the fifth, sea creatures.

Adam gave each one a name, and whatever he called them became their name. Over those days, he saw every kind of animal, both male and female, but he remained alone—there was no companion for him.

Then the Lord said to us, "It is not good for man to be alone. Let us make a helper for him."

So, God put Adam into a deep sleep. While he slept, God took one of his ribs and used it to create a woman. Then He closed the place where the rib had been removed.

When Adam woke up on the sixth day, God brought the woman to him. Adam immediately recognized her and said, "She is part of me—bone of my bones, flesh of my flesh. She will be called 'woman' because she was taken from man."

This is why a man leaves his parents and joins his wife, and the two become one.

Adam was created in the first week, and in the second week, the woman—made from his rib—was brought to him. God showed her to him, and because of this, a command was given: if a woman gives birth to a boy, she will be unclean for seven days, but if she gives birth to a girl, she will be unclean for fourteen days.

After Adam had lived in the land where he was created for forty days, we took him to the Garden of Eden so he could take care of it. His wife was brought into the Garden on the eightieth day, and from then on, they lived there together.

For this reason, a law was written on the heavenly tablets: "When a woman has a son, she will be unclean for seven days, just like the first week. Then, for thirty-three more days, she must stay away from anything holy and cannot enter the sacred place until her purification is complete."

If she has a daughter, she will be unclean for two weeks, just like the first two weeks, and will need sixty-six more days to complete her purification, making a total of eighty days.

Once these eighty days are over, she may enter the holy place again, because the Garden of Eden is holier than the rest of the earth, and every tree in it is sacred.

This is why the law was given regarding childbirth: a woman must not touch anything holy or enter the sacred place until her purification is complete.

This law was recorded for Israel so they would follow it for all generations.

During the first week of the first jubilee, Adam and his wife lived in the Garden of Eden for seven years. They took care of it, following the instructions they were given. Adam worked hard, and though he was naked, he felt no shame. He protected the garden from birds, animals, and livestock. He gathered fruit and saved some for himself and his wife.

After exactly seven years, in the second month, on the seventeenth day, the serpent approached the woman. It asked, "Did God really say you cannot eat from any tree in the garden?"

The woman replied, "We can eat from any tree except the one in the middle. God said, 'Do not eat from it or even touch it, or you will die.'"

The serpent said, "You won't die. God knows that if you eat it, your eyes will be opened, and you will be like gods, knowing good and evil."

The woman looked at the tree and saw that its fruit looked good to eat, was beautiful, and seemed to bring wisdom. She took some, ate it, and gave some to Adam. He ate as well.

Immediately, their eyes were opened, and they realized they were naked. They sewed fig leaves together to cover themselves.

God cursed the serpent, giving it eternal punishment. Then He turned to the woman and said, "Because you listened to the serpent and ate the fruit, I will greatly increase your pain in childbirth. You will suffer when you have children. You will long for your husband, and he will rule over you."

To Adam, He said, "Because you listened to your wife and ate from the tree I told you not to eat from, the ground is now cursed. You will have to work hard to get food from it for the rest of your life. It will produce thorns and weeds, and you will eat the plants of the field. You will sweat as you work for your food until the day you return to the ground. You were made from dust, and you will return to dust."

Then God made clothes from animal skins for Adam and his wife and dressed them. After that, He sent them out of the Garden of Eden.

On the day Adam left the garden, he offered a sacrifice at sunrise, burning fragrant spices like frankincense, galbanum, and stacte to seek forgiveness for his shame.

That same day, all animals, birds, and creatures that moved on the earth became silent. Before this, they had all spoken the same language. Then God sent all the creatures out of the Garden of Eden, separating them into their proper places. Of all the living things, only Adam was given clothing to cover his nakedness.

This is why it is written on the heavenly tablets that all who know the law's judgment must cover themselves and not expose their bodies as the other nations do.

On the new moon of the fourth month, Adam and his wife left the Garden of Eden and settled in the land of Elda, the place where they were created. Adam named his wife Eve.

During the first jubilee, they had no children. Later, Adam was with his wife, and he worked the land just as he had been taught in the Garden of Eden.

# Chapter IV.

During the third week of the second jubilee, Eve gave birth to Cain. In the fourth week, she had Abel, and in the fifth week, she gave birth to their daughter, Âwân.

In the first year of the third jubilee, Cain killed Abel because God accepted Abel's offering but rejected his. Cain attacked Abel in a field, spilling his blood, which cried out to heaven for justice.

God confronted Cain about his crime, and as a result, Cain was cursed and became a wanderer. He had to live with the guilt of his brother's death. This is why it is written on the heavenly tablets: "Cursed is anyone who kills their neighbor in secret, and all who hear of it must say, 'So be it.' Those who stay silent share in the guilt."

This is why we confess all our sins before the Lord—whether they happen in heaven, on earth, in the open, or in secret—so that nothing remains hidden. Adam and Eve mourned Abel for many years. But in the fourth year of the fifth week, their sadness turned to joy when Adam was with his wife again, and she gave birth to Seth. Adam said, "God has given us another child to take Abel's place."

In the sixth week, Eve had a daughter named Azûrâ. Cain married his sister Âwân, and by the end of the fourth jubilee, she gave birth to their son, Enoch. In the first year of the first week of the fifth jubilee, people began building houses on the earth. Cain built a city and named it after his son, Enoch. Adam and Eve had nine more sons.

During the fifth week of the fifth jubilee, Seth married his sister Azûrâ, and in the fourth year of the sixth week, they had a son named

Enos. Enos was the first to call on the name of the Lord.

In the third week of the seventh jubilee, Enos married his sister Nôâm, and in the third year of the fifth week, they had a son named Kenan. At the end of the eighth jubilee, Kenan married his sister Mûalêlêth, and in the third year of the first week of the ninth jubilee, they had a son named Mahalalel.

During the second week of the tenth jubilee, Mahalalel married Dinah, the daughter of Barakiel, who was his cousin. In the sixth year of the third week, they had a son named Jared.

During Jared's time, a group of angels called the Watchers came down to teach people about justice and judgment. In the eleventh jubilee, Jared married Baraka, the daughter of Râsûjâl, another relative. In the fifth week of that jubilee, she gave birth to Enoch.

Enoch was the first to learn writing, wisdom, and knowledge. He studied the signs in the sky, helping people understand time and seasons. He recorded the weeks, years, and Sabbaths exactly as they were revealed to him. He also received visions of past and future events, writing them down for future generations.

In the twelfth jubilee, during the seventh week, Enoch married Edna, the daughter of Danel, his cousin. In the sixth year of that week, they had a son named Methuselah.

Enoch spent six jubilees with the angels of God, learning about heaven and earth. He wrote everything down and warned against the Watchers, who had taken human wives. Because of his righteousness, God took Enoch away from the world and placed him in the Garden of Eden, where he recorded His judgments.

Later, God sent a flood to cleanse the earth because of human wickedness. Enoch's life stood as a warning to people. He also burned incense on a mountain, offering sweet-smelling spices to God. The Lord established four sacred places on earth: the Garden of Eden, the Mount of the East, Mount Sinai, and Mount Zion. These places would one day be made holy again to cleanse the world from its corruption.

In the fourteenth jubilee, Methuselah married Edna, the daughter of Azrial, his cousin. During the third week, in the first year of that week, she gave birth to Lamech.

In the fifteenth jubilee, Lamech married Betenos, the daughter of Baraki'il, his cousin. They had a son named Noah. Lamech said, "This child will bring us relief from the hardship caused by the cursed ground."

At the end of the nineteenth jubilee, during the seventh week of the sixth year, Adam died. His sons buried him in the land where he had been created. He lived 930 years but did not reach 1,000. According to the heavenly record, 1,000 years is like one day, so the prophecy about the tree of knowledge was fulfilled: "On the day you eat from it, you will die." In God's time, Adam died within that same "day."

That same year, Cain was killed when his house collapsed on him. This fulfilled what was written on the heavenly tablets: "Whoever kills with a weapon will be killed by the same." Since Cain killed Abel with a stone, he also died under stones as a just punishment.

In the twenty-fifth jubilee, Noah married Emzârâ, the daughter of Râkê'êl, his cousin. She gave birth to three sons: Shem in the third year, Ham in the fifth year, and Japheth in the first year of the sixth week.

# Chapter V.

When the number of people on earth increased and they had daughters, the angels of God noticed how beautiful they were. During a certain year in a jubilee, they chose wives for themselves from among them, taking whoever they wanted. Their children grew into giants, and soon, lawlessness spread across the land. Corruption filled the world as humans, animals, and birds became violent, attacking and even eating each other. People's thoughts became completely evil, and wrongdoing took over everywhere.

God saw how wicked the world had become. All living creatures had strayed from His ways, and the earth was filled with sin. Because of this, He decided to destroy mankind and every living thing He had created. But Noah stood apart—he was righteous, and God looked upon him with favor.

God's anger also turned toward the angels He had sent to earth. He stripped them of their power and commanded that they be chained deep underground, cut off from the rest of creation. Their giant offspring were also condemned to die. God declared that they would be wiped out by the sword and removed from the earth. He said, "My Spirit will not remain with humans forever, for they are mortal. Their lifespan will now be 120 years." Then, He caused violence to spread among the people, making them turn against each other until they were completely destroyed.

The fallen angels, forced to watch their children die, were imprisoned in the depths of the earth. There they will remain until the final judgment when God will punish all those who corrupted the world. No one escaped judgment. The wicked were completely removed from the earth. Afterward, God gave a new, pure nature to all living creatures so they would not turn back to evil.

The heavenly tablets record the laws for all creation. It is written that anyone who strays from their rightful path will be judged. Every action—whether done in heaven, on earth, in darkness, in light, in the depths, or even in Sheol—is seen by God. He is a just judge who does not show favoritism or accept bribes. If He has decided on a judgment, He will carry it out completely.

However, God also promised that if Israel repents and turns back to Him, He will forgive their sins. Once a year, He will grant mercy to those who admit their guilt and change their ways. But those who became corrupt before the flood were given no mercy. Only Noah was accepted by God, and his righteousness saved not only himself but also his sons. He followed all of God's instructions exactly as he was told.

God decided to destroy everything on earth—humans, animals, and birds. He commanded Noah to build an ark to survive the flood. Noah obeyed, constructing the ark just as God had instructed. This happened in the twenty-seventh jubilee, during the fifth week, in the fifth year, on the new moon of the first month. In the sixth year, during the second month, Noah and the animals entered the ark. On the seventeenth evening, the Lord shut the door from the outside.

Then, God opened the seven floodgates of heaven and the seven deep springs of the earth. For forty days and nights, heavy rain poured down, and water gushed up from the ground. The floodwaters rose until they covered even the tallest mountains by fifteen cubits. The ark floated on the surface of the waters. For five months—150 days—the flood remained over the earth. Finally, the ark came to rest on Mount Lubar, one of the mountains in the Ararat range.

In the fourth month, the deep springs of the earth were sealed shut, and the floodgates of heaven were closed. By the seventh month, the waters began to drain into the earth's depths. In the tenth month, the mountain peaks became visible again. By the first month of the new year, the land started to dry. On the seventeenth day of the second month, the ground was completely dry. Then, on the twenty-seventh day, Noah opened the ark, letting all the animals, birds, and creatures go free to return to the land.

# Chapter VI.

On the first day of the third month, Noah left the ark and built an altar on the mountain. He made a sacrifice to cleanse the earth, taking a young goat and using its blood to remove the guilt of the land. Everything that once lived on the earth had been wiped out, except for those saved in the ark with Noah. He placed the fat of the sacrifice on the altar and also offered an ox, a goat, a sheep, young goats, salt, a turtledove, and a young pigeon. He poured oil over them, sprinkled wine, and burned frankincense, creating a pleasing aroma that rose to God.

The Lord smelled the offering and made a promise to Noah, vowing never to destroy the earth by a flood again. He said that planting and harvest, cold and heat, summer and winter, day and night would continue as they were meant to, without interruption. Then He told Noah, "Have many children and fill the earth. I have placed all animals on land, in the sea, and in the sky under your authority. Just as I gave you plants to eat, I now give you everything. But do not eat meat that still has blood in it, because life is in the blood. Anyone who takes another person's life will be held accountable, for humans were made in God's image. Be fruitful and spread across the earth."

Noah and his sons made a vow before God that they would never eat blood. This became a lasting agreement for all future generations. God commanded that Israel remember this covenant, just as He later instructed Moses on the mountain. They were to sprinkle blood as part of their worship and never eat blood from any animal, bird, or livestock. This law was given as a permanent reminder so that Israel would always keep this commandment. Anyone who ate blood would be cut off from the land, and their descendants would be forgotten before God.

To seal His promise, God gave Noah a sign—He placed a rainbow in the clouds as a symbol of His eternal covenant that He would never again flood the earth to destroy it. It was also recorded in the heavenly tablets that a special festival, the Feast of Weeks, would be celebrated every year in this month to renew the covenant. This festival had been observed in heaven from the creation of the world until Noah's time, lasting 26 jubilees and five weeks of years. Noah and his sons continued to celebrate it for seven jubilees and one week of years until Noah died. After that, people forgot about it until Abraham revived it. His son Isaac, then Jacob, and their descendants observed it until Moses renewed it on the mountain.

God commanded the people of Israel to keep this festival in every generation, celebrating it as a reminder of the covenant. It became known as both the Feast of Weeks and the Feast of Firstfruits, a special day written into the law. It was established that this festival would be celebrated on a specific day each year, and Moses was given instructions on how it should be observed, ensuring that the Israelites would keep it faithfully for generations.

The new moons of the first, fourth, seventh, and tenth months were also set as days of remembrance, marking the changing seasons and the divisions of the year. Noah established these days as lasting feasts. On the new moon of the first month, he was told to build the ark, and on that same day, the earth became dry after the flood. On the new moon of the fourth month, the deep springs of the earth were sealed shut. On the new moon of the seventh month, the earth's abysses opened, allowing the floodwaters to drain. On the new moon

Translated by Tim Zengerink

of the tenth month, the mountain peaks became visible, and Noah rejoiced. These days were recorded in the heavenly tablets and were meant to be remembered forever.

The year was divided into four seasons, each lasting 13 weeks, making a total of 52 weeks. This cycle was written and established in the heavenly tablets and was not to be changed. The Israelites were commanded to follow a 364-day year, so the feasts and seasons would remain in their correct order. Any changes to this system would throw the years out of sync, leading to confusion about the feasts, new moons, Sabbaths, and the seasons.

God warned Moses that after his death, the Israelites would eventually stray from this system. They would abandon the 364-day calendar, causing their festivals, holy days, and Sabbaths to fall out of order. Some would begin following the lunar calendar, leading to mistakes in their observances and making holy days unclean. They would mix the sacred with the ordinary, forget the commandments, and even start eating blood and all kinds of meat without following the laws.

This message was given as a warning, so the Israelites would not be led astray and so they would understand the serious consequences of ignoring the appointed times and the laws of the covenant.

# Chapter VII.

In the seventh week of the first year of this special time, Noah planted vineyards on the mountain where the ark had landed—Mount Lubar, one of the Ararat Mountains. It took four years for the vines to grow and produce grapes. In the seventh month of that year, Noah gathered the grapes.

Noah made wine from the grapes and stored it in a container. He kept it until the fifth year, and on the first day of the first month, he held a big feast. As part of the celebration, he made a burnt offering to God, sacrificing a young ox, a ram, seven one-year-old sheep, and a young goat to ask for forgiveness for himself and his sons.

Noah started with the goat, using some of its blood and meat on the altar. He placed all the fat on the altar as part of the burnt offering. Then, he did the same with the ox, the ram, and the sheep, placing their meat and fat on the altar and mixing them with oil. He poured wine over the fire and burned incense. The smell rose up and pleased God.

Noah and his sons enjoyed the feast, drinking the wine with joy. As the evening came, Noah went to his tent, fell asleep, and became drunk. While he was asleep, he accidentally uncovered himself and lay naked.

His son Ham saw him like this and went to tell his brothers. But Shem and Japheth took a garment, placed it on their shoulders, and walked backward into the tent to cover their father without looking at him.

When Noah woke up and realized what had happened, he cursed Ham's son, Canaan, saying, "Canaan will be a servant to his brothers." Then he blessed Shem, saying, "Praise be to the Lord, the God of Shem. May Canaan serve him." He also prayed for Japheth, saying, "May God bless Japheth and let him live among Shem's people. And may Canaan be his servant too."

Ham was upset when he heard the curse on his son. He left Noah and went with his sons—Cush, Mizraim, Put, and Canaan—to build a city, naming it after his wife, Ne'elatama'uk.

Japheth, feeling jealous, built his own city and named it after his wife, 'Adataneses.

Shem, however, stayed close to Noah and built a city near him on the mountain, calling it Sedeqetelebab, after his wife.

This is how three cities were built near Mount Lubar: Sedeqetelebab in the east, Na'eltama'uk in the south, and 'Adataneses in the west.

The sons of Shem were Elam, Asshur, Arpachshad (who was born two years after the flood), Lud, and Aram. Japheth's sons were Gomer, Magog, Madai, Javan, Tubal, Meshech, and Tiras. These were the children and grandchildren of Noah.

In the twenty-eighth jubilee, Noah began teaching his grandsons the laws and commands he had received. He told his sons to live good and honest lives, to dress modestly, respect their Creator, honor their parents, love their neighbors, and avoid evil and impurity.

He warned them that the flood had come because of three great sins: wickedness, impurity, and the wrongdoing of the Watchers, who had taken wives from among human women.

These sins led to the birth of the Nephilim, who became violent and corrupt. The Giants killed the Nephilim, the Nephilim killed the Eljo, and the Eljo turned against humans. The world became filled with wickedness, violence, and bloodshed.

People didn't just harm one another; they also hurt animals, birds, and all living creatures. Blood covered the earth, and people's hearts became filled with evil thoughts and wicked plans.

Because of this, God wiped everything off the face of the earth. Every living thing was destroyed because of the violence and corruption.

Noah then spoke to his sons, saying, "I see what you are doing, and it worries me. You are not following the right path. You are becoming jealous of one another, arguing, and growing apart. I fear that after I die, you will start shedding blood, and because of this, you too will be removed from the earth.

Anyone who kills another person or drinks animal blood will be destroyed. Their family line will end, and they will have no descendants. Those who do such things will go to Sheol, a place of punishment and darkness, and they will be taken from the earth.

The killing of people and animals must stop. Any blood spilled must be covered because I have been commanded to warn you, your children, and all creatures.

Do not let your hearts be stained by the flesh of animals, for blood is life, and God will hold everyone accountable for the blood they shed. The earth cannot be cleansed of spilled blood unless the one who caused it also sheds their own blood. Only then will the land be pure.

Now, my children, listen to me. Live righteously and fairly, so that you will always walk in the right way. If you do good, your actions will rise before God, who saved me from the flood.

Go and build cities, plant trees, and grow crops. When you plant fruit trees, do not pick the fruit for the first three years. In the fourth year, the fruit will be holy, and the first portion should be given to God, the Creator of heaven and earth.

The remaining fruit will be for those who serve God. In the fifth year, you may harvest the fruit freely, and everything you plant will grow well.

This rule was first given by Enoch, the ancestor of your forefathers. Methuselah passed it down to his son Lamech, and Lamech taught me, just as their ancestors had taught them.

Now, I am passing this rule to you, just as Enoch gave it to his son long ago. He carefully taught his children and grandchildren, ensuring they followed it throughout their lives."

# Chapter VIII.

In the first week of the twenty-ninth jubilee, at the very beginning, Arpachshad married Rasu'eja, the daughter of Susan, who was Elam's daughter. Three years later, they had a son named Kainam. As Kainam grew older, his father taught him how to write. One day, Kainam went out to look for a place to build a city. While exploring, he found an old inscription carved into a rock by earlier generations. He read what was written, copied it down, and unknowingly committed a sin. The inscription contained secret knowledge from the Watchers—beings who had studied the movements of the sun, moon, and stars to find hidden signs in the sky. Fearing Noah's anger, Kainam kept this discovery a secret.

In the first year of the second week of the thirtieth jubilee, Kainam married Melka, the daughter of Madai, who was Japheth's son. Four years later, they had a son named Shelah, who said, "I have truly been sent." In the fifth week of the thirty-first jubilee, Shelah married Mu'ak, the daughter of Kesed, his father's brother. Five years later, she gave birth to a son named Eber. Later, in the thirty-second jubilee, during the seventh week, Eber married 'Azûrâd, the daughter of Nebrod. In the sixth year of that week, they had a son named Peleg. He was given this name because, during his lifetime, Noah's descendants started dividing the land among themselves. They first made a secret agreement on how to split it, then told Noah about their decision.

At the start of the thirty-third jubilee, in the first year of the first week, the earth was officially divided into three regions: one for Shem, one for Ham, and one for Japheth. This division was made under the guidance of a messenger sent by God. Noah's descendants and their families gathered to decide the borders of each territory.

Shem's land was in the middle of the earth, and he and his descendants were meant to live there forever. His territory started at the middle of the Rafa mountains, where the Tina River begins. It stretched west along the river to the waters of the deep and flowed into the Sea of Me'at, then continued toward the Great Sea. Japheth's land was to the north of Shem's, while Ham's land lay to the south. Shem's territory extended south to Karaso and followed the western coastline of the Great Sea until it reached the mouth of the Egyptian Sea. From there, it went down the shores of the Great Sea to 'Afra, then reached the Gihon River. It followed the southern banks of the river eastward, passing just below the Garden of Eden. His land included Eden, the eastern regions, and all the way back to the Rafa mountains and the Tina River. This area, including the lands of Eden, was Shem's permanent inheritance.

Noah was pleased with this division because it matched the blessing he had spoken: "Blessed be the Lord God of Shem, and may the Lord dwell in his land." He knew that the Garden of Eden was the holiest place on earth, where God's presence was. He also knew that Mount Sinai, in the wilderness, and Mount Zion, at the center of the earth, were sacred places made to align with each other. Noah praised God for His wisdom and power and recognized the special blessing given to Shem and his descendants. Shem's land included Eden, the Red Sea region, India, the lands surrounding the Red Sea, and mountain ranges like Bashan, Lebanon, Sanir, Amana, Asshur, and Elam, as well as the Ararat region. This large territory was rich and full of resources.

Ham's land was located south of the Garden of Eden, beyond the Gihon River. His territory stretched to the fiery mountains and reached the 'Atel Sea. It extended west to the sea of Ma'uk, where many lost things eventually ended up. From there, it moved north to Gadir, followed the Great Sea's coastline, and circled back to the Gihon River, returning near the Garden of Eden. This land was given to Ham and his descendants as their permanent inheritance.

Japheth's land was north of the Tina River and covered the northern and northeastern regions, stretching all the way to the land of Gog. It extended eastward to the Qelt mountains and the sea of Ma'uk, then curved toward Gadir and beyond. To the west, it reached Fara, then turned toward 'Aferag before extending east to the Sea of Me'at. Japheth's land continued northeast, reaching the Tina River and the Rafa mountains. His territory was vast and included five large islands. Japheth's land was known for its cold climate, while Ham's land was hot, and Shem's land had a balanced, temperate climate in between.

# Chapter IX.

Ham divided his land among his sons. Cush received the first portion, which was in the eastern region. To the west of Cush was Mizraim's land, followed by Put's territory even farther west. The farthest west, along the seacoast, was the land given to Canaan.

Shem also divided his inheritance among his sons. Elam received the first portion, which covered the land east of the Tigris River and stretched further east, including all of India. His territory also included the coastline along the Red Sea, the waters of Dedan, the mountains of Mebri and Ela, the land of Susan, and the regions near Pharnak, reaching the Red Sea and the Tina River.

The second portion was given to Asshur, which included all the land of Assyria, along with the cities of Nineveh and Shinar, as well as the borderlands of India. This region followed the path of the major rivers in the area.

The third portion went to Arpachshad, covering the entire land of the Chaldeans, east of the Euphrates River, near the Red Sea. His inheritance also included the desert lands near the sea's mouth facing Egypt, along with Lebanon, Sanir, and 'Amana, extending to the Euphrates River.

The fourth portion was given to Aram. His land was located between the Tigris and Euphrates Rivers, north of the Chaldean territory, and stretched to the Asshurite mountains and the land of 'Arara.

Lud, Shem's fifth son, received the mountains of Asshur and the surrounding lands. His territory extended to the Great Sea and stretched eastward, toward the land of his brother Asshur.

Japheth also distributed his land among his sons. Gomer received the first portion, which stretched eastward from the northern region to the Tina River. To the north, Magog's land included the inner northern territories, extending toward the Sea of Me'at.

Madai's land was located west of his brothers' territories and included islands and coastal regions.

Javan, who received the fourth portion, was given all the islands and lands that bordered Lud's territory.

Tubal received the fifth portion, which covered the central landmass bordering Lud. His land extended to the second landmass and stretched beyond into the third section of land.

Meshech was given the sixth portion, which extended beyond the third landmass and reached the eastern border of Gadir.

Tiras received the seventh portion, which included four large islands located in the sea. These islands extended toward the border of Ham's land. The Kamaturi Islands were also assigned to the descendants of Arpachshad as part of their inheritance.

Noah's sons divided the earth among their descendants while Noah was still alive. He made them take an oath, binding them under a curse so that no one would take land that was not given to them.

They all agreed and swore, saying, "So be it, so be it," for themselves and for their future generations. This agreement was meant to last forever, until the day of judgment. On that day, the Lord will judge all nations with fire and the sword for their sins, their corruption, and the evil they have spread across the earth.

# Chapter X.

During the third week of that jubilee, unclean spirits began leading Noah's descendants astray, causing confusion and destruction. Noah's sons came to him, troubled by how these demons were deceiving, blinding, and even killing their children.

Noah prayed to the Lord, saying:

"God of all spirits, You have shown mercy to me and my family, saving us from the flood and sparing us from the fate of the wicked. Your kindness and compassion have been great.

Please continue Your grace upon my sons. Do not let these evil spirits take control of them or lead them to destruction. Bless me and my children so that we may grow in number and fill the earth. You know how the Watchers, the ancestors of these spirits, acted in my time. Bind these spirits and keep them in the place of punishment so they cannot harm Your faithful servants. They were created for destruction and should not have power over those who seek righteousness.

Do not let them rule over the living or the righteous, for only You have authority over all spirits. Do not allow them to overpower those who choose to walk in Your ways forever."

The Lord heard Noah's prayer and ordered us to bind the spirits. Then, Mastema, the leader of these spirits, stepped forward and said:

"Lord, Creator of all, allow some of them to remain with me to carry out my commands. Without them, I cannot fulfill my purpose of testing and corrupting mankind, for their wickedness is great."

The Lord replied:

"I will allow one-tenth of them to remain with you, but the other nine-tenths must be bound in the place of punishment."

The Lord then commanded one of us to teach Noah how to heal diseases, knowing that mankind would continue to act wickedly. We obeyed, binding the evil spirits and leaving only one-tenth under Mastema's control on earth. We also taught Noah how to use herbs from the earth to heal sickness and resist the temptations brought by these spirits. Noah wrote everything down in a book, recording all the remedies and instructions we gave him. This knowledge helped protect his descendants from harm.

Noah passed these teachings to his eldest son, Shem, whom he loved most. After living a righteous life, Noah died and was buried on Mount Lubar in the land of Ararat. He lived for 950 years, completing 19 jubilees, two weeks, and five years. Among all men, he was the most righteous, second only to Enoch, who served as a testimony for future generations until the day of judgment.

During the thirty-third jubilee, in the first year of the second week, Peleg married Lomna, the daughter of Sina'ar. In the fourth year, she gave birth to a son, Reu. Peleg said, "Look, the people have become wicked, for they have begun to build a city and a tower in the land of Shinar."

The people had moved away from the land of Ararat and settled in Shinar. There, they decided to build a great city and a tower that would reach the heavens. They said, "Let's build a tower so high that we will make a name for ourselves." They worked for 43 years, making bricks and using asphalt from the sea as mortar. The tower rose to an incredible height of 5,433 cubits and 2 palms, with its walls extending 13 and 30 stades.

The Lord said, "They are one people with a single language, and now nothing they plan will be impossible for them. Let us go down and confuse their language so they will not understand one another."

We went down with the Lord to see the city and the tower. He confused their language, making them unable to continue their work. The land of Shinar was called Babel because the Lord scattered the people across the earth. A powerful wind knocked the tower down, and its ruins remained between Asshur and Babylon in Shinar. The people were dispersed in the first year of the thirty-fourth jubilee.

Ham and his sons moved to their assigned land in the south. However, Canaan saw the land of Lebanon, from the river of Egypt, and found it desirable. Instead of settling in the land given to him by the sea, he chose to stay in Lebanon, east and west of the Jordan and along the coast.

Ham, along with Cush and Mizraim, warned Canaan:

"You have taken land that does not belong to you. This land was given to Shem and his descendants. If you stay here, you and your children will be cursed and driven out for your disobedience. Do not live in Shem's territory, for it was assigned to him and his descendants by God."

But Canaan ignored them and remained in Lebanon, from Hamath to the borders of Egypt, along with his sons. That is why the land became known as Canaan.

Japheth and his sons moved to their rightful land by the sea. However, Madai did not like his assigned territory. He asked Ham, Asshur, and Arpachshad for a piece of their land. He settled in Media, near his brother-in-law, and named the land after himself. The name Media has remained ever since.

# Chapter XI.

During the thirty-fifth jubilee, in the third week of its first year, Reu married a woman named Ôrâ, the daughter of Ûr, who was the son of Kesed. In the seventh year of that week, she gave birth to a son named Serôh. Around this time, Noah's descendants started fighting among themselves. They captured and killed each other, spilling human blood across the land. Some even began eating blood. They built fortified cities, walls, and towers. People became proud, forming the first kingdoms and waging wars—city against city, nation against nation. Weapons were created, children were trained in warfare, and men started capturing others to sell as slaves.

Ûr, the son of Kesed, built the city of Ara in the land of the Chaldees, naming it after himself and his father. The people made molten idols and began worshiping them. They carved statues and created impure images. Evil spirits led them further into sin, and Mastêmâ, the ruler of these spirits, worked tirelessly to spread corruption. He sent his demons to commit all kinds of wickedness, violence, and bloodshed. Because of the widespread sin during this time, Serôh was later called Serug, a name reflecting the transgressions of that era.

Serug grew up in Ur of the Chaldees, near his wife's mother's family. Sadly, he also worshiped idols. During the thirty-sixth jubilee, in the first year of the fifth week, Serug married Melka, the daughter of Kaber, who was the daughter of his father's brother. In the first year of that week, she gave birth to a son named Nahor. Nahor was raised in Ur of the Chaldees, where his father taught him the ways of their people, including astrology and fortune-telling.

During the thirty-seventh jubilee, in the first year of the sixth week, Nahor married 'Ijaska, the daughter of Nestag from the Chaldees. In the seventh year of that week, they had a son named Terah. During this time, Mastêmâ sent flocks of ravens and birds to destroy crops and steal seeds before they could be planted. As a result, Terah's name was given to symbolize the hardship caused by the ravens. The land became barren, and people struggled to gather enough food from their harvests.

In the thirty-ninth jubilee, during the first year of the second week, Terah married Edna, the daughter of Abram, who was his father's sister. In the seventh year of that week, she gave birth to a son, whom they named Abram, after his grandfather, who had died before his birth.

As Abram grew older, he began to see the mistakes and wickedness of the world. He noticed that the people around him worshiped idols and practiced unclean rituals. His father taught him how to write, but by the time he was 14, Abram chose to distance himself from his father's ways to avoid idol worship. Instead, he prayed to the Creator of all things, asking for guidance to live a pure and righteous life.

When the season for planting arrived, people gathered in the fields to guard their seeds from the ravens. Although he was still a boy, Abram went with them. When a massive flock of ravens came to eat the seeds, Abram ran toward them and shouted, "Do not come down! Go back to where you came from!" Miraculously, the ravens turned away. That day, Abram drove the ravens away seventy times, and not a single bird remained in the land where he lived.

The people were amazed and word of Abram spread throughout the Chaldees. That year, farmers sought his help, and he guided them during the planting season. With his assistance, they successfully sowed all their seeds. That year, the harvest was abundant, and the people rejoiced.

In the first year of the fifth week, Abram invented a new tool for oxen plows to prevent ravens from stealing the seeds. He designed a wooden container that attached to the plow, allowing seeds to drop directly into the soil as the oxen moved. This clever invention prevented birds from eating the seeds before they could grow. The people quickly adopted Abram's design, and soon, they were able to plant and harvest without fear of the birds. Abram's wisdom and leadership brought prosperity and peace to the land.

# Chapter XII.

During the sixth week, in the seventh year, Abram spoke to his father, Terah, and said, "Father!"

Terah answered, "I am here, my son."

Abram asked, "Why do you worship and bow down to these idols? They have no life, no spirit, and they only lead people astray. Why put your trust in them?

Worship the God of heaven, the One who sends rain and dew, who controls everything on earth, and who created all things with His word. All life comes from Him.

Why believe in lifeless statues made by human hands? You carry them on your shoulders, yet they cannot help you. They bring shame to those who make them and deceive those who worship them. Do not follow them."

Terah replied, "I know what you are saying is true, my son, but what can I do? The people here force me to serve these idols. If I speak against them, they will kill me because they are committed to worshiping them. Stay silent, my son, or they will kill you too."

Abram shared these thoughts with his brothers, but they became angry with him. So he remained quiet.

During the fortieth jubilee, in the second week and the seventh year, Abram married Sarai, his father's daughter, and she became his wife. His brother Haran also married in the third year of the third week, and in the seventh year, his wife gave birth to a son named Lot. Their other brother, Nahor, also took a wife.

When Abram was sixty years old, in the fourth week and the fourth year, he woke up in the middle of the night and set fire to the house of idols, burning everything inside. No one knew he had done it. When the people awoke, they rushed to save their gods from the fire. Haran tried to rescue them, but the flames overtook him, and he died in Ur of the Chaldees in front of his father, Terah. They buried him there.

After this, Terah left Ur with his sons and traveled toward the land of Lebanon and Canaan. He settled in Haran, where Abram stayed with him for fourteen years.

During the sixth week, in the fifth year, Abram stayed awake on the new moon of the seventh month to observe the stars and predict the coming rainfall. As he watched, he thought, "All the movements of the stars, the moon, and the sun are in the hands of the Lord. Why am I searching for answers in them?

If God wills, He sends rain in the morning and evening. If He chooses, He withholds it. Everything happens according to His will."

That night, Abram prayed, saying, "My God, the Most High, You are my only God, and I have chosen to follow You alone. You created everything, and all that exists is the work of Your hands.

Protect me from the evil spirits that mislead people so that I will not be led away from You. Strengthen me and my descendants forever, so we will never turn from Your ways."

Then he asked, "Should I return to Ur of the Chaldees, where they are calling me back? Or should I stay here? Guide me, O God, and make my path clear so that I do not follow my own desires."

After Abram finished praying, the word of the Lord came to him, saying:

"Leave your land, your people, and your father's house, and go to the land I will show you. I will make you into a great and mighty nation.

I will bless you and make your name great, and through you, all the families of the earth will be blessed. I will bless those who bless you and curse those who curse you.

Do not be afraid, for I will be your God forever, for you and your descendants through all generations."

The Lord also commanded, "Open his mouth and ears so that he may understand and speak the language I have given." This was the original language of creation, which had not been spoken since the Tower of Babel. At that moment, Abram's mouth, ears, and lips were opened, and the Lord spoke to him in Hebrew.

Abram then took the writings of his ancestors, which were written in Hebrew, and copied them, studying them carefully. The Lord helped him understand what he could not comprehend, and Abram spent six months of the year studying these writings during the rainy season.

In the seventh year of the sixth week, Abram told his father that he planned to leave Haran to visit the land of Canaan and return later.

Terah said to him, "Go in peace. May the eternal God guide you, protect you from harm, and grant you grace, mercy, and favor in the eyes of those you meet. May no one have the power to hurt you. Go safely.

If you find a land that pleases you, take me with you, and take Lot, the son of your brother Haran, as your own. But leave Nahor, your brother, with me. When you return safely, we will all go with you."

# Chapter XIII.

Abram left Haran with his wife Sarai and his nephew Lot, traveling to the land of Canaan. On the way, they passed through Asshur and arrived at Shechem, where they settled near a large oak tree. The land was beautiful, stretching from Hamath to the great oak. Then, the Lord appeared to Abram and said, "I will give this land to you and your future family." Abram built an altar there and made a burnt offering to God.

After that, Abram moved to a mountain between Bethel in the west and Ai in the east, where he set up his tent. He saw that the land was rich and full of life, with vineyards, fig trees, pomegranates, olive trees, cedars, date palms, and many other plants. Water flowed from the mountains, making the land fertile. Abram gave thanks to the Lord, who had guided him safely from Ur of the Chaldees to this land of blessings.

In the first year of the seventh week, on the first day of the first month, Abram built an altar on the mountain and prayed, saying, "You are the eternal God, and You are my God." He offered a burnt sacrifice, asking God to always be with him. Then, Abram traveled south and arrived in Hebron, where a city was being built. He stayed there for two years before moving further south to Bealoth. While he was there, a famine spread across the land.

In the third year of that time, Abram went to Egypt and stayed for five years. During his stay, Pharaoh took Sarai into his palace. But the Lord sent terrible plagues upon Pharaoh and his household because of her. As a result, Abram became very wealthy, gaining many sheep, cattle, donkeys, horses, camels, servants, silver, and gold. His nephew Lot also became rich.

Pharaoh returned Sarai to Abram and sent them out of Egypt. Abram traveled back to the place where he had first set up his tent, between Bethel and Ai, near the altar he had built before. There, he thanked the Lord for bringing him back safely. In the forty-first jubilee, during the third year of the first week, Abram made another burnt offering at the altar and prayed, saying, "You are the Most High God, and You are my God forever."

In the fourth year of that time, Lot separated from Abram and moved to Sodom, where the people were extremely sinful. Abram was saddened by Lot's choice, especially since he had no children of his own. Later that year, after Lot was taken captive, the Lord spoke to Abram and said, "Look around in every direction—north, south, east, and west. I will give all this land to you and your descendants forever. Your family will be as numerous as the dust of the earth. Walk through the land, for it will belong to you and your future generations."

Abram then moved to Hebron and settled there. That same year, Chedorlaomer, the king of Elam, joined forces with Amraphel, the king of Shinar, Arioch, the king of Sellasar, and Tergal, the king of the nations. Together, they attacked the king of Gomorrah. The king of Sodom fled, and many people were wounded in the Siddim Valley near the Salt Sea. The invading kings took over Sodom, Adam, and Zeboim, capturing Lot and taking all his belongings to Dan.

One of the survivors escaped and told Abram what had happened to Lot. Abram quickly gathered his trained servants, armed them, and went after the enemy. He successfully rescued Lot, recovered his possessions, and brought back the people who had been taken. After the victory, Abram gave one-tenth of the recovered goods to the Lord, establishing a lasting rule that a tenth of all produce—grain, wine, oil, cattle, and sheep—should be given to the priests who serve before God.

The king of Sodom then approached Abram, bowed before him, and said, "Lord Abram, keep the goods for yourself, but return the people you rescued to me." Abram replied, "I swear to the Most High God that I will take nothing from you—not even a thread or a sandal strap—so that you cannot say, 'I made Abram rich.' The only things I will take are what my men have already eaten and the share that belongs to Aner, Eschol, and Mamre, who helped me. They will receive their portion."

## Chapter XIV.

In the fourth year of that time, on the first day of the third month, the Lord spoke to Abram in a vision, saying, "Do not be afraid, Abram. I am your protector, and your reward will be very great." Abram replied, "Lord, what can You give me if I still have no children? The one who will inherit everything I own is Eliezer of Damascus, the son of my servant Maseq. You have not given me any children of my own."

The Lord answered, "Eliezer will not be your heir. You will have a child of your own, and he will inherit everything." Then, the Lord took Abram outside and said, "Look up at the sky and try to count the stars, if you can." As Abram looked at the endless stars above him, the Lord said, "That is how many descendants you will have." Abram believed what the Lord had promised, and because of his faith, God considered him righteous. Then the Lord said, "I am the one who brought you out of Ur of the Chaldees to give you this land as your inheritance forever. I will be your God and the God of your descendants."

Abram asked, "Lord, how can I be sure that I will inherit this land?" The Lord told him, "Bring Me a three-year-old cow, a three-year-old goat, a three-year-old ram, a turtledove, and a young pigeon." Abram did as the Lord commanded. In the middle of the month, he stayed near the oak trees of Mamre, close to Hebron. There, he built an altar, sacrificed the animals, and poured their blood on it. He cut the animals in half and placed the pieces across from each other, but he did not divide the birds. Then, large birds came down, trying to eat the sacrifices, but Abram chased them away.

As the sun began to set, Abram fell into a deep sleep. A heavy darkness surrounded him, filling him with fear. Then, the Lord spoke, saying, "Know for certain that your descendants will live in a land that is not their own. They will be enslaved and mistreated for 400 years. But I will punish the nation that enslaves them, and in the end, they will leave with many possessions. You, however, will live in peace and grow old before being buried. In the fourth generation, your descendants will return to this land, for the sins of the Amorites are not yet complete."

When Abram woke up, the sun had already set. He saw a blazing fire and a cloud of smoke pass between the divided pieces of the sacrifice. That day, the Lord made a covenant with Abram, saying, "I will give this land to your descendants—from the river of Egypt to the great river, the Euphrates. This land belongs to the Kenites, Kenizzites, Kadmonites, Hittites, Perizzites, Rephaim, Amorites, Canaanites, Girgashites, and Jebusites."

Abram completed the offerings, including the birds and their grain and drink offerings, which were burned in the fire. The Lord sealed His covenant with Abram on that day, just as He had done with Noah in this same month. Abram renewed the festival and the practice as a tradition for himself and his future generations.

Overjoyed, Abram shared everything that had happened with his wife, Sarai. He believed fully in God's promise that he would have many descendants. However, Sarai still had not been able to conceive. She told Abram, "Take my Egyptian maid, Hagar, as your wife. Maybe I can have children through her." Abram listened to Sarai and agreed. She gave Hagar to Abram as his wife. He was with Hagar, and she became pregnant and gave birth to a son. Abram named him Ishmael. This happened in the fifth year of that time, when Abram was 86 years old.

# Chapter XV.

In the fifth year of the fourth week of this special time, during the third month, Abraham celebrated the Festival of First Fruits from the grain harvest. He made offerings to God on the altar, presenting the first portion of his crops. He sacrificed a young cow, a goat, and a sheep as burnt offerings, along with grain and drink offerings, and sprinkled frankincense on the altar.

The Lord appeared to Abraham and said, "I am God Almighty. Follow My ways and live with honesty and integrity. I will make a covenant with you and greatly increase your descendants." Abraham bowed down to the ground, and God continued, "My covenant is with you, and you will become the ancestor of many nations. From now on, your name will no longer be Abram but Abraham, because I have made you the father of many nations. I will bless you abundantly, and your family will grow. Nations and kings will come from you. This covenant will last forever between Me and your descendants. I will be your God and the God of your future generations. I will give you and your family the land of Canaan, where you now live as foreigners, as a permanent possession, and I will be their God."

Then God gave Abraham instructions, saying, "You and your descendants must keep My covenant for all generations. Every male among you must be circumcised as a sign of this agreement. On the eighth day after birth, every male must be circumcised, whether he was born in your household or bought from a foreigner. This will be a permanent mark of the covenant between us. Any male who is not circumcised on the eighth day has broken My covenant and will be cut off from his people."

God also said, "As for your wife, she will no longer be called Sarai. Her name will now be Sarah. I will bless her, and she will give birth to a son. She will be the mother of nations, and kings will come from her." Abraham bowed down and laughed to himself, thinking, "How can a hundred-year-old man have a child? Can Sarah, at ninety years old, give birth?" Then Abraham said to God, "If only Ishmael could receive Your blessing!"

But God replied, "No, Sarah will give you a son, and you will name him Isaac. My everlasting covenant will be with him and his descendants. As for Ishmael, I have heard your request. I will bless him, make him fruitful, and give him many descendants. He will become the father of twelve rulers, and I will make him into a great nation. But My covenant will be with Isaac, whom Sarah will give birth to at this time next year."

After God finished speaking, He left. Abraham immediately obeyed God's command. That same day, he circumcised Ishmael, every male in his household—whether born there or bought—and himself. Every male in his household was circumcised that day as a sign of the covenant. The commandment to circumcise boys on the eighth day was recorded as a permanent law on the heavenly tablets. Anyone who failed to do this would be removed from the covenant and separated from God's people.

All the angels who serve in God's presence were created to worship Him, and God chose Israel as His special people even before they existed. He declared that Israel would always be with Him and His holy angels. The children of Israel were commanded to keep this covenant forever. If they remained faithful, they would never be removed from their land. This law was given as an everlasting command.

Even though Ishmael and Esau were Abraham's descendants, God did not choose them to be near Him. He chose Israel, set them apart, and made them His people, different from all other nations. While every nation belongs to God, He placed spiritual rulers over them for guidance. But He reserved Israel for Himself, without any intermediaries. He alone is their God, leading and protecting them forever.

However, I must warn you that the children of Israel will not keep this covenant. They will fail to circumcise their sons, ignoring this eternal law, and will leave them uncircumcised as they were born. This will anger the Lord because they will have abandoned His covenant, rejected His laws, and followed the customs of other nations. Their rebellion and disrespect will lead to their exile, and they will be cast out of their land. There will be no forgiveness for them because they will have broken this everlasting covenant.

# Chapter XVI.

At the start of the fourth month, under the shade of the large oak at Mamre, we visited Abraham. We told him that his wife, Sarah, would have a son. Sarah, listening nearby, laughed quietly to herself because she didn't believe it was possible. We reassured her and told her not to be afraid, though she denied laughing. Still, we revealed that her son's name, Isaac, had already been written in the heavenly records. We promised that when we returned at the right time, she would be expecting a child.

During that same time, the Lord brought judgment upon Sodom, Gomorrah, Zeboim, and the surrounding areas near the Jordan. Fire and sulfur rained down, destroying them completely. To this day, those cities remain in ruins. Their wickedness had reached its limit, as they had corrupted themselves and spread evil everywhere. Just as Sodom was punished, so will any place that follows in their footsteps.

However, God showed mercy to Lot because of Abraham. He rescued Lot from the destruction, but even after escaping, Lot and his daughters committed a terrible sin—something unheard of since the time of Adam. Their actions were recorded as a serious wrongdoing in the heavenly records. Because of this, it was decided that Lot's descendants would not survive. Just like Sodom, his family line would be cut off. Their judgment is certain, and when the time comes, none of them will remain.

That same month, Abraham left Hebron and traveled toward the area between Kadesh and Shur. He settled in the mountains near Gerar. By the middle of the fifth month, he moved again, this time to the Well of the Oath. Then, in the middle of the sixth month, as promised, the

Lord visited Sarah, and she became pregnant. Just as God had said, Sarah gave birth to a son in the third month, on the day of the Festival of First Fruits of the Harvest. And so, Isaac was born, fulfilling God's promise.

We told Abraham that while his other sons would be connected to different nations, Isaac's descendants would be set apart as a holy people, chosen by God. His family line would belong to the Most High, forming a special kingdom and priesthood devoted to serving Him. After delivering this message, we left Abraham and went to Sarah, sharing the same words with her. Both Abraham and Sarah rejoiced deeply at this news.

Abraham built an altar to honor the Lord, who had protected him and blessed him with great joy, even though he was living in a foreign land. At the altar near the Well of the Oath, he held a seven-day festival of celebration. During this time, he made temporary shelters for himself and his household. This was the first time the Feast of Tabernacles was observed on earth. Every day for seven days, Abraham made offerings to the Lord, including two oxen, two rams, seven sheep, and one male goat as a sin offering, asking for forgiveness for himself and his descendants.

Along with these offerings, he also gave thanksgiving sacrifices, which included seven rams, seven goats, seven sheep, and seven male goats, as well as grain and drink offerings. He burned all the fat on the altar as a pleasing aroma to the Lord. Every morning and evening, Abraham burned incense made from a special blend of spices: frankincense, galbanum, stacte, nard, myrrh, costus, and other fragrant spices. He combined them in equal amounts to create a pure and sweet-smelling incense for God.

For the full seven days, Abraham joyfully celebrated the festival with complete devotion. His entire household took part in the observance, but no outsiders or uncircumcised people were allowed to join. Abraham praised God, giving thanks for creating him and guiding him according to His divine plan. God already knew that Abraham's descendants would follow the path of righteousness, and from his family would come a holy people who reflected His goodness.

With joy and respect, Abraham honored God and named this celebration the "Festival of the Lord," a time of rejoicing that pleased the Most High. We blessed Abraham and his descendants forever because he followed the festival exactly as it was written in the heavenly records. Because of this, it was decided in the heavenly writings that Israel would celebrate the Feast of Tabernacles every year for seven days in the seventh month. This was to be a lasting commandment for all generations.

This festival would never be forgotten. It was established that Israel must observe it every year. They were instructed to live in temporary shelters, wear wreaths on their heads, and take leafy branches and willow branches from the streams. Abraham gathered palm branches and beautiful fruits, and each morning, he walked around the altar seven times, giving thanks and praising God with great joy for all that He had done.

# Chapter XVII.

In the first year of the fifth week of that special time, Isaac was weaned, and Abraham held a great feast in the third month to celebrate. Ishmael, the son of Hagar the Egyptian, stood beside Abraham, and Abraham felt great joy. He praised God for giving him sons and not leaving him without children. He also remembered the promise God had made to him when Lot had separated from him, and his heart was full of gratitude as he gave thanks to the Creator.

However, Sarah saw Ishmael playing and dancing while Abraham was celebrating, and she became jealous. She said to Abraham, "Get rid of this slave woman and her son. Her son will not share in the inheritance with my son, Isaac." Abraham was deeply troubled by this because it involved both his servant and his son.

But God spoke to Abraham and said, "Do not be distressed about the boy or the maidservant. Listen to what Sarah is saying, because your descendants will come through Isaac. But do not worry—I will also make a great nation from the son of the slave woman because he is your child too."

The next morning, Abraham got up early, took some bread and a skin of water, placed them on Hagar's shoulder along with her son, and sent them away.

Hagar wandered in the wilderness of Beersheba. When the water ran out, the child became weak and collapsed. She placed him under the shade of an olive tree and walked a short distance away, saying, "I cannot bear to watch my child die." She sat down and wept.

Then an angel of God appeared to her and said, "Hagar, why are you crying? Get up, take the child, and hold him, for God has heard your cries and seen your child's suffering." Suddenly, Hagar saw a well of water. She quickly filled the water skin and gave the boy a drink. Then, they continued on to the wilderness of Paran. The boy grew up and became an excellent archer, and God was with him. Later, Hagar found him a wife from Egypt, and she gave birth to a son. He named him Nebaioth, saying, "The Lord was near to me when I called upon Him."

In the first year of the seventh week, on the twelfth day of the first month, voices from heaven spoke about Abraham. They declared that

52

he had been faithful in everything God had commanded him, that he truly loved the Lord, and that he had proven his loyalty in every test.

Then Mastêmâ, the adversary, came before God and said, "Abraham may love You, but he loves his son Isaac even more. Command him to offer Isaac as a burnt sacrifice on the altar, and then You will see if he is truly obedient. Then You will know if he is faithful in everything."

But the Lord already knew Abraham's heart and that he was strong through every test. God had already tested him when He called him to leave his homeland, when he faced famine, when he encountered the riches of kings, and when his wife was taken from him. God tested him when He gave him the covenant of circumcision and again when he had to send Ishmael and Hagar away. Through all these trials, Abraham remained faithful and patient. He never hesitated to follow God's instructions because he loved the Lord and was completely devoted to Him.

## Chapter XVIII.

One day, God called out, "Abraham, Abraham!" and Abraham answered, "Here I am." Then God said, "Take your son, Isaac—the one you love—and go to the high mountains. There, on a mountain that I will show you, offer him as a burnt sacrifice."

Early the next morning, Abraham got up, saddled his donkey, and took two of his servants along with Isaac. He cut the wood for the burnt offering and set out for the place God had told him about. After traveling for three days, he saw the mountain in the distance.

When they arrived at a well, Abraham said to his servants, "Stay here with the donkey. Isaac and I will go up the mountain to worship. After we have worshiped, we will come back to you."

Abraham took the wood for the offering and placed it on Isaac's shoulders. He himself carried the fire and the knife as they walked together toward the mountain.

On the way, Isaac spoke to his father, saying, "Father?" Abraham replied, "Yes, my son?" Isaac asked, "We have the fire and the wood, but where is the lamb for the burnt offering?"

Abraham answered, "God will provide the lamb for the sacrifice, my son." And the two of them continued on.

When they reached the place God had chosen, Abraham built an altar and arranged the wood on it. Then, he tied up Isaac and placed him on the altar, on top of the wood. Abraham reached for the knife and was about to sacrifice his son.

At that moment, I was there, along with Mastêmâ, and we heard God call out, "Abraham, Abraham!" Abraham quickly responded, "Here I am." God said, "Do not harm the boy. Now I know that you truly respect and obey Me, because you were willing to offer your son, your only son."

Then, I called out to Abraham from heaven again, saying, "Abraham, Abraham!" He answered, "Here I am." I told him, "Do not lay a hand on the boy. You have shown your deep trust in God by not holding back your son from Him."

Mastêmâ was left in shame. Abraham looked up and saw a ram caught by its horns in the bushes. He went over, took the ram, and offered it as a sacrifice in place of Isaac.

Abraham named that place "The Lord Will Provide," and even today, people say, "On the mountain of the Lord, it will be provided."

Then God called out to Abraham again from heaven and said, "I swear by Myself," declares the Lord, "Because you have done this and did not hold back your beloved son, I will bless you greatly. I will make your descendants as numerous as the stars in the sky and the grains of sand on the shore. They will conquer the cities of their enemies, and through your descendants, all the nations of the earth will be blessed, because you have obeyed My voice. You have proven your faithfulness in everything I have asked of you. Now go in peace."

Abraham returned to his servants, and together they traveled back to Beersheba, where he settled near the Well of the Oath.

From that time on, Abraham celebrated this event every year for seven days with great joy. He named it the Festival of the Lord, remembering the seven days of his journey and safe return.

It is recorded in the heavenly writings that Israel and its future generations must observe this festival every year for seven days, celebrating with joy.

# Chapter XIX.

In the first year of the first week of the forty-second jubilee, Abraham returned and settled near Hebron, in a place called Kirjath Arba. He lived there for fourteen years.

In the first year of the third week, Sarah passed away in Hebron. Abraham mourned for her and arranged her burial. During this time, he was tested to see if he would remain patient and free from anger, and he passed the test by staying calm and composed.

He kindly approached the sons of Heth and asked for a burial place for his wife. The Lord made them favor him, and they treated him with respect. Abraham asked for the field that contained the cave near Mamre, also known as Hebron. They agreed to give it to him for four hundred pieces of silver. Even though they offered it as a gift, Abraham insisted on paying the full price. After completing the purchase, he bowed before them twice and buried Sarah in the cave.

Sarah lived for 127 years—two jubilees, four weeks, and one year in total. Her passing was Abraham's tenth test of faith, and he remained faithful and patient. Even though God had promised him the land, he still humbly asked for a burial site instead of questioning God's promise. Because of his faith, he was honored in the heavenly records as a friend of God.

In the fourth year of that time, Abraham arranged a marriage for Isaac. He chose Rebecca, the daughter of Bethuel, who was the son of Nahor, Abraham's brother. Around the same time, Abraham also married another wife, Keturah, who came from the daughters of his servants. Hagar had already passed away before Sarah. Over the next fourteen years, Keturah gave birth to six sons: Zimram, Jokshan, Medan, Midian, Ishbak, and Shuah.

In the second year of the sixth week, Rebecca gave birth to twin sons, Jacob and Esau. Jacob was quiet and righteous, living peacefully in tents, while Esau was wild, spending his time hunting in the fields and becoming skilled in battle. Abraham loved Jacob, but Isaac favored Esau.

As Abraham watched Esau's behavior, he realized that Jacob, not Esau, would carry on his name and legacy. He called Rebecca, knowing she loved Jacob more than Esau, and said:

"My daughter, take great care of Jacob,
For he will inherit my place on this earth.
He will bring blessings to all people
And will bring honor to the line of Shem.

The Lord has chosen him to be His own people,
    Set apart from all the nations of the earth.
Though Isaac loves Esau more,
    You love Jacob, and I ask you to care for him even more.

Let your love for him guide your actions,
    For he will bring blessings to us
    And to all future generations.

Be strong and take joy in your son Jacob,
    For I have loved him more than all my children.

He is blessed forever,
    And his descendants will fill the earth.
If a man could count the grains of sand on the earth,
    Jacob's descendants would be just as many.

All the blessings God has given me
    Will belong to Jacob and his descendants forever.
Through his family, my name and the names of my ancestors—
    Shem, Noah, Enoch, Mahalalel, Enos,
    Seth, and Adam—will be honored.

These blessings will uphold the heavens,
    Strengthen the earth,
And renew the stars above."

Then Abraham called Jacob to stand before Rebecca and kissed him. He blessed him, saying:

"My beloved son Jacob, whom I cherish,
    May God bless you from the heavens above.

May He give you all the blessings He gave to Adam, Enoch,
    Noah, and Shem.
May all the promises He made to me and our family be fulfilled in
    you,
And may those blessings last forever, as long as the heavens
    remain above the earth.
May no spirit of Mastêmâ have power over you or your
    descendants,
    To lead you away from the Lord your God,
    From this day forward and forever.

May the Lord be your Father,
    And may you be His firstborn son,
    A blessing to His people for all time.

Go in peace, my son."

After this, Abraham and Jacob spent time together, and Rebecca loved Jacob with all her heart, far more than Esau. However, Isaac continued to favor Esau, loving him more than Jacob.

# Chapter XX.

In the forty-second jubilee, during the first year of the seventh week, Abraham gathered his family together. He called Ishmael and his twelve sons, Isaac and his two sons, and the six sons of Keturah along with their children.

Abraham taught them to follow the ways of the Lord, to live with honesty and kindness, and to treat others with fairness and justice. He urged them to stay true to God's commandments, never turning away from them. He warned them to avoid all kinds of immoral and impure behavior and to make sure such actions did not take place in their families or communities.

He stressed that if any woman or girl among them committed an immoral act, she should be punished, and no one should desire her or seek her out. He also warned them not to marry the daughters of Canaan because the people of Canaan would one day be removed from the land.

He reminded them about the punishment that came upon the giants and the people of Sodom. He described how they were destroyed because of their wickedness, their sins, and the corruption they spread.

Stay away from sin and anything unclean,
  And always choose to do what is right.
Do not bring shame to our family,
  Or disgrace to your own lives.

Do not let your children suffer violence,
  Or bring a curse upon yourselves like Sodom,
  Or have your descendants punished like the people of
  Gomorrah.

My sons, I urge you to love the God of heaven,
  And follow all His commandments.

Do not be led astray by false gods or their wicked ways.
Do not make idols for yourselves,
  For they are useless and lifeless,
  Created by human hands, and trusting in them is trusting in
  nothing.

Do not bow down to them or serve them,
  But worship the Most High God and honor Him always.

Seek His favor and strive to do what is right,
  So that He may be pleased with you, show you kindness,
  And send rain for your fields in the morning and evening.

May He bless the work of your hands,
  Bless your food and water,
  Bless your children and your land,
  And bless your animals and flocks.

You will be a blessing to the world,
  And all nations will look to you with honor.
They will bless your children in my name,
  So they too may receive the same blessings I have been given.

Abraham gave gifts to Ishmael and his sons, as well as to the sons of Keturah. Then, he sent them away from Isaac, giving all that he owned to Isaac.

Ishmael and his sons, along with the sons of Keturah and their families, traveled together and settled in the lands stretching from Paran to the entrance of Babylon, covering the eastern regions near the desert. Over time, they intermarried and became known as the Arabs and the Ishmaelites.

# Chapter XXI.

In the sixth year of the seventh week of this jubilee, Abraham called his son Isaac and said,"My son, I have grown old, and I do not know how much time I have left. I am now 175 years old, and my life has been full. Throughout the years, I have always remembered the Lord and done my best to follow His ways with all my heart. I have lived with honesty and integrity. I have rejected idols and those who worship them. My heart and soul have been fully devoted to obeying my

Creator, for He is the one true God—holy, faithful, and completely just. He does not show favoritism or accept bribes. He judges fairly and will hold accountable those who break His laws or abandon His covenant.

Now, my son, follow His commandments, obey His instructions, and live according to His laws. Stay away from anything sinful or unclean, especially idol worship. Never eat the blood of any animal, whether from cattle, birds, or any other creature. If you offer a peace sacrifice, do it properly. Pour its blood on the altar and burn its fat along with fine flour mixed with oil and a drink offering. These will create a pleasing aroma to the Lord. When offering a thanksgiving sacrifice, burn the fat from the belly, the inner organs, the kidneys, and the fat near the loins and liver. Place these parts on the fire of the altar along with the meat and the drink offering as a sweet-smelling sacrifice to the Lord.

Eat the meat on the same day or the next, but never on the third day. If any remains until then, it is no longer acceptable and must not be eaten. Anyone who eats it on the third day commits a sin. I have read these instructions in the writings of our ancestors, in the words of Enoch and Noah. Also, always sprinkle salt on your offerings. The salt of the covenant must never be missing from any sacrifice you bring before the Lord.

When choosing wood for sacrifices, only use these kinds: cypress, bay, almond, fir, pine, cedar, savin, fig, olive, myrrh, laurel, or aspalathus. Pick wood that is strong, fresh, and looks good. Do not use wood that is cracked, dark, or damaged. Never use old wood, as it has lost its fragrance and will not create a pleasing aroma before the Lord. Apart from the types I've mentioned, do not use any other kind, as they do not produce a sweet scent.

Follow these instructions carefully, my son, so that you will do what is right in all things. Keep yourself clean at all times. Wash with water before approaching the altar. Wash your hands and feet before and after offering a sacrifice. Make sure no blood remains on your body or clothes. Be careful when handling blood—always cover it with dust. Never eat blood, for it holds the life of the creature. Do not consume any blood at all.

Never accept money or bribes in exchange for a person's life, so that innocent blood is not shed without justice. When blood is spilled, the land becomes polluted, and it can only be cleansed by the blood of the one responsible. Do not take payment to excuse the taking of a life. A life must be paid for with life so that you remain right before the Lord, the Most High God, who protects those who do good. May He shield you from evil and save you from all harm.

My son, I have seen that people's actions are full of sin and wickedness. Their ways are unclean, filled with evil and corruption. There is no righteousness among them. Be careful not to follow their ways or imitate their behavior. Do not commit sins that lead to death before the Most High God. If you do, He will turn away from you, allow you to fall into your own wrongdoing, and remove you and your descendants from the land. Your name and family line will be erased from the earth.

Stay far from their sinful ways and unclean actions. Follow the laws of the Most High God, obey His will, and live righteously in all things. If you do this, He will bless your work and raise a righteous family from you for generations to come. Your name and mine will never be forgotten under heaven and will last forever.

Go in peace, my son. May the Most High God—my God and your God—give you strength to do His will. May He bless your descendants and all future generations with righteousness so that you and your family will be a blessing to the whole earth."

With that, Abraham departed, his heart full of joy.

# Chapter XXII.

In the second year of the first week of the forty-fourth jubilee, the same year Abraham passed away, Isaac and Ishmael traveled from the Well of the Oath to celebrate the Feast of Weeks—the festival of the first fruits of the harvest—with their father, Abraham. Seeing both of his sons together made Abraham very happy. Isaac, who owned a lot of land in Beersheba, often visited his property before returning to his father. Around that time, Ishmael also came to visit, and the two brothers reunited.

Isaac offered a burnt sacrifice on the altar that Abraham had built in Hebron. He also presented a thank offering and shared a joyful feast with his brother Ishmael. Rebecca baked fresh cakes from the new grain and gave them to Jacob to bring to Abraham so he could eat and bless the Creator before his passing. Isaac also sent a generous thank offering with Jacob for Abraham to enjoy. Abraham ate and drank, then praised the Most High God, saying:

"Blessed is the Creator of heaven and earth,
Who made all the good things of this world,
And gave them to people,
So they may eat, drink, and give thanks to their Creator."

Then he continued, "I thank You, my God, for letting me see this day. I am now 175 years old, and my life has been full. I have lived in peace, and no enemy has been able to harm me in all that You have given to me and my children. My God, may Your kindness and peace be with me and my descendants. May they be a chosen people, set apart as Yours among all the nations for generations to come."

Then Abraham called Jacob and said, "My son Jacob, may the God who created everything bless you and give you the strength to live righteously and follow His ways. May He choose you and your descendants to be His people forever. Come closer, my son, and give me a kiss."

Jacob stepped forward and kissed him, and Abraham said:

"Blessed be my son Jacob,
    And blessed be all the children of the Most High God
    forever.
May God give you righteous descendants,
    And may He choose some of your children to be holy among
    the nations.
May other nations serve you,
    And may all people respect your family.
Be strong in the presence of others,
    And lead the descendants of Seth.
Through you, righteousness will continue,
    And you will become a holy nation."


"May the Most High God bless you with all the blessings
    He gave to me, to Noah, and to Adam.
May these blessings remain with your descendants forever.
May He cleanse you from all sin and impurity,
    Forgiving any wrongs you have done without knowing.
May He strengthen and bless you.
May you inherit the whole earth,
    And may He renew His covenant with you,
    Making you His chosen people forever.

May He always be your God,
     And the God of your descendants,
     In truth and righteousness, for all time."


"Remember my words, my son Jacob,
     And always follow the commandments of your father,
     Abraham.
Do not mix with the other nations.
Do not eat with them or follow their customs.
Do not form close friendships with them,
     For their ways are corrupt and sinful.
They worship the dead and follow evil spirits.
They even eat meals near graves,
     And their actions are meaningless.
They do not understand,
     And they say to a piece of wood, 'You are my god,'
And to a stone, 'You are my lord and savior.'
They are blind to the truth of their own actions."


"My son Jacob, may the Most High God guide and bless you.
May He keep you away from their wickedness and sinful ways.
Do not marry any of the daughters of Canaan,
     For their descendants are doomed to destruction.
Because of Ham's sin, the line of Canaan will be completely
     wiped out.
None of them will be saved on the Day of Judgment.
Idol worshipers and those who live in impurity
Will have no place in the land of the living.
They will be forgotten on earth
     And sent to Sheol, the place of judgment,
     Just like the people of Sodom, who were completely
     destroyed."

"Do not be afraid, my son Jacob.
Be strong, my child, a descendant of Abraham.
May the Most High God protect you from harm
And rescue you from evil.
This house I have built carries my name on the earth,
    And it belongs to you and your descendants forever.
It will be known as the house of Abraham.
You will honor my name before God forever,
    And your descendants will carry my name
Through all generations of the earth."

After Abraham finished blessing Jacob and giving him instructions, they lay together on one bed. Jacob rested in Abraham's arms, and Abraham kissed him seven times, filled with love and joy for his grandson. With all his heart, he blessed Jacob, saying:

"May the Most High God, the Creator of all things,
    Who brought me out of Ur of the Chaldees to inherit this
    land forever,
    Bless my holy descendants. Blessed be the Most High
    forever."

Then he said to Jacob, "My dear son, who brings me great joy, may God's kindness and grace always be with you and your children. May He never leave you or turn away from you. May His eyes always watch over you and your family. May He protect and bless you, choosing you as His own people. May He give you every lasting blessing, renewing His promise with you and your descendants for generations to come, according to His perfect plan."

# Chapter XXIII.

Jacob rested in Abraham's arms, unaware that his grandfather had passed away. Abraham gently placed two of Jacob's fingers over his eyes, blessed the God of all gods, covered his own face, stretched out his feet, and peacefully passed away, joining his ancestors.

When Jacob woke up, he noticed that Abraham's body was cold, like ice. Alarmed, he cried out, "Grandfather, Grandfather!" But there was no response. Realizing that Abraham had died, Jacob quickly ran to his mother, Rebecca, and told her what had happened. Rebecca then went to Isaac in the night and informed him. Together with Jacob, who carried a lamp, they entered the room and found Abraham lying still, lifeless.

Isaac fell over his father's body, weeping with deep sorrow, and kissed him. Soon, the entire household was filled with the sound of mourning. Ishmael, Abraham's son, also arrived and wept for his father. Everyone in the house grieved together, crying loudly from the depths of their hearts.

Later, Isaac and Ishmael buried Abraham in the cave near his wife, Sarah. For forty days, the men of the household mourned him. This included Isaac, Ishmael, their sons, and the sons of Keturah, each grieving in their own places. When the mourning period ended, it was recorded that Abraham had lived a total of 175 years—three jubilees and four weeks of years. He had lived a full life and passed away peacefully, satisfied with his years.

In the past, people had lived much longer—up to nineteen jubilees—but after the Flood, lifespans began to shorten. No one lived that long anymore, as people aged faster, suffered more hardships, and faced the increasing wickedness of the world. Abraham was different, living a life pleasing to God, blameless in his actions. Yet, even he did not reach four full jubilees because of the growing evil on earth, which shortened his days.

From that time forward, human lifespans would continue to decrease. By the time of the final judgment, people would no longer live for even two full jubilees. As they aged, their knowledge would fade, and their understanding would weaken. A man who lived a jubilee and a half would be considered old, yet most of his life would be filled with hardship, sorrow, and suffering, with little peace.

Disaster would come one after another—wounds upon wounds, trouble upon trouble, and endless bad news. People would suffer from sickness, famine, exhaustion, war, captivity, and countless other struggles. These misfortunes would fall upon a generation filled with wickedness, a generation whose actions were sinful and corrupt.

In those days, people would complain, saying, "Our ancestors lived long and good lives—up to a thousand years. But now, we only live seventy or eighty years if we are strong, and our days are full of suffering. There is no peace in this evil generation."

Children would turn against their parents and elders, blaming them for their troubles. They would abandon the covenant that the Lord had made with their ancestors, refusing to follow His commandments or walk in His ways. They would completely turn away from God, caring only about themselves.

Everyone would chase after evil, and every word spoken would be full of lies. Their actions would be corrupt and disgusting, leading only to destruction. The earth would suffer because of their wickedness— vineyards would dry up, oil would disappear, and their unfaithfulness would bring ruin. Humanity, along with animals, livestock, birds, and sea creatures, would suffer because of the sins of mankind.

People would rise up against each other—young against old, the poor against the rich, the humble against the powerful, and beggars against rulers—all because they had abandoned the law and the covenant. They would forget the sacred commandments, the holy festivals, the Sabbaths, the jubilees, and all of the Lord's instructions.

Armed with weapons, they would fight in the hope of finding righteousness again, but they would never return to the right path until the earth was covered in blood. One person would turn against another in endless violence. Even those who survived would refuse to change. Instead, they would be filled with pride and greed, seeking only to take from others. They would claim the name of the Lord but live without truth or righteousness, corrupting even the most sacred places with their sin.

A great punishment would fall upon this generation. The Lord would allow them to fall into war, captivity, and suffering. He would bring ruthless foreign nations against them—people without mercy, who would not spare the old or the young. These invaders would be more wicked and powerful than any before them, bringing destruction to Israel and committing terrible sins against Jacob's descendants.

The land would be covered in blood, and there would be no one left to bury the dead.

In those days, people would cry out for help, calling for rescue from sinners and oppressors, but no one would come to save them.

The heads of children would turn gray with age,
> And even babies as young as three weeks old would appear as old as men of a hundred years,
> Worn down by suffering and endless hardship.

Yet in those days, some would begin to seek the Lord again.

Children would study the law,
> Search for the commandments,
> And return to the path of righteousness.

Lifespans would grow longer,
    And people would once again live for many years,
    Almost reaching a thousand years,
    Just as in the days of old.

No one would be considered old,
    And no one would feel like their life was too short.
Everyone would have the strength of youth and the joy of
    childhood.

Their days would be filled with peace and happiness,
    For Satan and all evil forces would be removed from the
    earth.
Blessings and healing would fill their lives.
In that time, the Lord would restore health to His people,
    And they would rise up in joy,
    Driving away their enemies.

The righteous would celebrate with gratitude,
    Lifting their voices in endless praise to the Lord,
    Witnessing His justice and the defeat of their enemies.

Their bodies would rest in the earth,
    But their spirits would rejoice forever,
    Knowing that the Lord is a just and merciful judge,
    Showing kindness to all generations who love Him.

Then the Lord said to Moses, "Write down these words, for they are recorded on the heavenly tablets as a message for future generations."

# Chapter XXIV.

In the first year of the third week of the forty-fourth jubilee, after Abraham passed away, the Lord blessed his son Isaac. Isaac left Hebron and moved to live near the Well of the Vision, where he stayed for seven years. In the first year of the fourth week, a famine struck the land, just like the one that had happened during Abraham's time.

One day, Jacob was cooking a pot of lentils when Esau came in from the fields, exhausted and starving. Esau said, "Give me some of that red stew." Jacob replied, "Sell me your birthright, and I will give you bread and stew." Esau thought, "I'm so hungry I could die—what good is my birthright to me?" So he agreed, swearing an oath and giving his birthright to Jacob. Jacob then gave him bread and stew, which Esau ate until he was full. Esau did not care about his birthright, and because of this, he was called Edom, named after the red stew for which he had traded his inheritance. From that moment on, Jacob became the rightful firstborn, and Esau lost his position.

When the famine ended, in the second year of that week, Isaac planned to go to Egypt but instead went to Gerar, where Abimelech, the king of the Philistines, ruled. The Lord appeared to Isaac and said, "Do not go to Egypt. Stay in the land I show you and live here. I will be with you and bless you. I will give this land to you and your descendants and fulfill the promise I made to Abraham, your father. I will make your family as numerous as the stars in the sky and give them all this land. Through your descendants, all nations will be blessed because Abraham listened to My voice, obeyed My commandments, and followed My laws. Now, you must do the same and remain here."

Isaac stayed in Gerar for 21 years. While he was there, Abimelech warned his people, "Anyone who harms Isaac or takes anything that belongs to him will be put to death." Isaac became successful among the Philistines, gaining many possessions, including oxen, sheep, camels, donkeys, and many servants. He planted crops in the Philistine land and harvested a hundred times more than expected, becoming very wealthy. This made the Philistines jealous.

Out of envy, the Philistines filled the wells that Abraham's servants had dug with dirt. Then Abimelech said to Isaac, "Leave us because you have become too powerful for us." So in the first year of the seventh week, Isaac moved to the valleys of Gerar. There, his servants reopened the wells that Abraham had dug, which the Philistines had filled after his death. Isaac named the wells just as his father had.

Isaac's servants dug a new well in the valley and found fresh water. But the shepherds of Gerar argued with them, saying, "This water belongs to us." So Isaac named the well "Dispute" because of their unfair claim. His servants dug another well, but the locals fought over it too, so he named it "Opposition."

Isaac then moved on and dug another well, and this time, no one fought over it. He named it "Room" and said, "The Lord has made space for us, and we have prospered in this land."

In the first year of the first week of the forty-fourth jubilee, Isaac moved to the Well of the Oath. That night, on the new moon of the first month, the Lord appeared to him and said, "I am the God of Abraham, your father. Do not be afraid, for I am with you. I will bless you and make your descendants as numerous as the sand of the earth because of My servant Abraham." Isaac built an altar at the same place where his father had built one. He called on the name of the Lord and offered a sacrifice. His servants then dug another well and found fresh water.

Later, Isaac's servants dug another well but found no water. They told Isaac, and he said, "I have sworn peace with the Philistines, and they know about this well." He named the place "Well of the Oath" because of the peace agreement he had made with Abimelech, Ahuzzath, and Phicol, the commander of their army. Isaac understood that he had no choice but to make peace with them.

On that day, Isaac cursed the Philistines, saying:

"The Philistines will be cursed until the day of judgment when they are scattered among the nations. They will be a disgrace and a curse, hated and punished by sinful nations and the Kittim. Even if they escape the enemy's sword and the Kittim, they will still face judgment from the righteous nation. They will remain enemies of my descendants forever. When the day of judgment arrives, their entire bloodline will be wiped out, and no one from the Caphtorim will be left on earth.

If they try to rise to power, they will be brought down. If they become strong, they will be uprooted. If they hide among other nations, they will be found and removed. If they descend into Sheol, they will suffer greatly and never find peace. If they are taken as captives, those who pursue them will destroy them before they can escape. No descendants will remain, and their name will be erased from history. They will be cursed forever."

This decree is written on the heavenly tablets and will be fulfilled on the day of judgment, when the Philistines will be completely wiped out from the earth.

# Chapter XXV.

In the second year of that week, during this jubilee, Rebecca called her son Jacob and said, "My son, do not marry one of the daughters of Canaan like your brother Esau. He has married two women from this land, and they have brought me nothing but sorrow. Their ways are immoral and sinful, and there is no goodness in them. Everything they do is filled with wickedness, and they bring only grief and pain.

I love you deeply, my son, and I bless you every moment, day and night. Please listen to me and follow my advice. Do not choose a wife from the women of this land. Instead, find a wife from my father's family, from among our own people. If you marry within our family, the Most High God will bless you, and your children will be righteous and holy."

Jacob answered his mother, "Mother, I am still young, only nine weeks old, and I have no knowledge or experience with women. I have not made any promises to anyone, and I do not plan to marry a daughter of Canaan.

I remember what our father Abraham told me. He warned me not to marry a woman from Canaan but to choose a wife from our own family and people. I know that your brother Laban has daughters, and I would like to marry one of them.

I have kept myself pure for this reason, staying away from sin and corruption. Father Abraham gave me clear instructions to avoid lust and wrongdoing, and I have followed his guidance.

Even though my brother Esau has pressured me many times to marry one of his wives' sisters, I have refused to follow his example. I promise you, mother, I will never marry a woman from Canaan, and I will not act wickedly as my brother has done.

Do not worry, mother. I will honor your wishes and live a righteous life, never straying from the right path."

Hearing this, Rebecca lifted her eyes to heaven, stretched out her hands, and prayed, thanking and praising the Most High God, the Creator of heaven and earth. She said,

"Blessed be the Lord God, and may His holy name be praised forever. He has given me Jacob, a pure son, a righteous seed. He belongs to You, Lord, and his descendants will be Yours for all generations to come.

Bless him, O Lord, and let my words carry the blessing of righteousness as I speak over him."

Then, filled with the spirit of righteousness, she placed her hands on Jacob's head and said,

"Blessed are You, Lord of righteousness and God of all ages. May You bless Jacob above all the people of the earth.

Guide him, my son, on the path of righteousness, and may his descendants also walk in truth and goodness.

May his children multiply like the months of the year and become as numerous as the stars in the sky, outnumbering the grains of sand by the sea.

Give them this good land, as You promised to Abraham and his descendants, and may they possess it forever.

May I live to see your children, my son, and may all your descendants be holy and blessed.

Just as you have brought me joy and comfort, may you be blessed by the womb that bore you, by the love of my heart, by the milk that nourished you, and by the words of my mouth that praise you always.

May you grow and spread across the earth, and may your descendants rejoice forever in heaven and on earth.

May your children be perfect, full of joy, and find peace on the great day of peace.

May your name and your family line last forever. May the Most

High God always be your God, and may the God of righteousness be with your descendants. Through them, may His holy place be established for all generations.

Blessed are those who bless you, and cursed are those who falsely curse you."

Rebecca kissed Jacob and said, "May the Lord of all creation love you as much as my heart loves you. May my joy and blessings always remain with you." Then, she finished her blessings.

# Chapter XXVI.

In the seventh year of that week, Isaac called his older son, Esau, and said, "My son, I am old, and my eyesight is failing. I do not know how much longer I will live. Take your bow and arrows, go to the fields, and hunt some wild game for me. Prepare my favorite meal and bring it to me so that I may eat and bless you before I die."

Rebecca overheard Isaac speaking to Esau. After Esau left early to hunt, she called Jacob and said, "I heard your father tell Esau, 'Go hunt for me and prepare my favorite meal so I can eat and bless you before the Lord before I die.' Now listen carefully, my son. Go to the flock and bring me two young goats. I will prepare them just the way your father likes. Then you will take the food to him, and he will eat and bless you before he dies. This way, you will receive the blessing instead."

Jacob hesitated and said, "But, Mother, what if my father recognizes my voice or touches me? I have smooth skin, and Esau is hairy. If he touches me, he will know I am tricking him, and instead of a blessing, I will bring a curse upon myself."

Rebecca replied, "Let any curse fall on me, my son. Just do what I tell you."

So Jacob obeyed and brought the two young goats. Rebecca prepared the food exactly how Isaac liked it. Then she took Esau's best clothes, which she had in the house, and dressed Jacob in them. She covered his hands and the smooth part of his neck with goat skins so that he would feel hairy like Esau. Then she handed Jacob the food and bread she had made.

Jacob went to his father and said, "Father, I have done as you asked. Please sit up and eat the meal I prepared so that you may bless me."

Isaac asked, "How did you find the game so quickly, my son?"

Jacob answered, "Because the Lord your God helped me succeed."

Isaac said, "Come closer so I can touch you, my son, and see if you really are Esau."

Jacob moved closer, and Isaac touched him. He said, "The voice is Jacob's, but the hands feel like Esau's." Isaac did not recognize him because his hands felt hairy like Esau's. It was by God's will that Isaac could not tell the difference, so he continued to bless him.

"Are you really my son Esau?" Isaac asked.

Jacob answered, "Yes, I am."

Isaac said, "Bring me the food so I may eat and bless you."

Jacob brought him the meal and wine, and Isaac ate and drank. Then Isaac said, "Come closer, my son, and kiss me."

When Jacob leaned in to kiss him, Isaac smelled the scent of Esau's clothes and blessed him, saying:

"My son smells like a field that the Lord has blessed.
May God give you rain from the sky,
    Rich soil,
    And plenty of grain and wine.

May nations serve you,
  And people show you honor.
Be a ruler over your brothers,
  And may your mother's sons respect you.

Anyone who curses you will be cursed,
  And anyone who blesses you will be blessed."

Just as Jacob left, Esau returned from his hunt. He prepared the meal and brought it to his father, saying, "Father, sit up and eat the venison I've brought so you can bless me."

Isaac asked, "Who are you?"

Esau replied, "I am your firstborn son, Esau."

Isaac trembled and said, "Then who was it that hunted game and brought it to me? I already ate it, and I have blessed him—and the blessing will stand!"

When Esau heard this, he let out a loud and bitter cry. "Father, bless me too!" he pleaded.

Isaac said, "Your brother came with deceit and took your blessing."

Esau cried out, "No wonder his name is Jacob! He has cheated me twice—first, he took my birthright, and now he has taken my blessing! Haven't you saved any blessing for me?"

Isaac replied, "I have made him lord over you and given him all his brothers as servants, along with plenty of grain and wine. What more can I give you, my son?"

Esau begged, "Father, do you only have one blessing? Bless me too!" And he wept loudly.

Isaac said,

"You will live far from the fertile land
    And without the blessing of rain from above.
You will survive by the sword
    And serve your brother.

But when you can no longer bear it,
    You will break free from his control.
However, your choices will lead to great sin,
    And your descendants will be lost."

Esau was filled with hatred toward Jacob because of the blessing his father had given him. He said to himself, "Soon my father will die, and then I will kill my brother Jacob."

# Chapter XXVII.

Rebecca had a dream warning her about Esau's plan to take revenge and kill Jacob. She immediately called Jacob and said, "Your brother Esau is planning to harm you. Listen to me, my son, and do what I say. Leave right away and go to my brother Laban in Haran. Stay there for a while until Esau calms down and forgets what happened. Then I'll send for you to return."

Jacob replied, "I'm not afraid of him. If he comes after me, I'll defend myself and fight back."

But Rebecca said, "I don't want to lose both of you in one day."

Jacob answered, "You know that Father is old and nearly blind. If I leave without his blessing, it will upset him, and he might curse me instead of bless me. I won't go unless he sends me himself."

Rebecca reassured him, "I will talk to him, and he will bless you before you leave."

She went to Isaac and said, "I am deeply troubled by Esau's wives. If Jacob marries a woman like them, I don't want to live anymore. The women of this land are full of wickedness."

Isaac then called Jacob, blessed him, and said, "Do not marry a woman from Canaan. Go to Mesopotamia, to your mother's family, and find a wife from the daughters of your uncle Laban. May God Almighty bless you, give you many children, and make you into a great nation. May He grant you the blessings promised to Abraham, and may you inherit this land, where you now live as a foreigner—the land God gave to Abraham. Go in peace, my son."

Isaac sent Jacob on his way, and Jacob traveled to Mesopotamia, to the house of Laban, the son of Bethuel, Rebecca's brother.

After Jacob left, Rebecca was filled with sorrow and wept for her son.

Isaac comforted her, saying, "Do not cry for Jacob, my love. He left in peace, and he will return in peace. The Most High God will watch over him, protect him, and guide him. He will succeed in all he does, and when he comes back, we will rejoice with him again. Be at ease, for Jacob is righteous and follows the path of truth. He will not perish. Wipe your tears."

Isaac's words reassured Rebecca, and they both blessed Jacob.

Jacob left the well of Beer-sheba and began his journey toward Haran in the first year of the second week of the 44th jubilee. He arrived at a place called Luz, later known as Bethel, on the new moon of the first month. As the sun was setting, he turned off the road and decided to spend the night there.

He took a stone from the area, placed it under his head as a pillow, and lay down to sleep.

That night, Jacob had a dream. He saw a ladder reaching from the ground up to heaven, with angels going up and down on it. At the top of the ladder stood the Lord, who spoke to him:

"I am the Lord, the God of your grandfather Abraham and the God of your father Isaac. The land where you are lying, I will give to you and your descendants. Your family will be as countless as the dust of the earth, spreading in all directions—west, east, north, and south. Through you and your descendants, all the families of the earth will be blessed.

I am with you and will protect you wherever you go. I will bring you back to this land, and I will not leave you until I have done everything I have promised."

When Jacob woke up, he said, "Surely, the Lord is in this place, and I didn't even realize it." Filled with awe, he added, "This place is amazing. It is truly the house of God and the gateway to heaven."

Early the next morning, Jacob took the stone he had used as a pillow, stood it upright as a pillar, and poured oil over it. He named the place Bethel, though it was originally called Luz.

Then Jacob made a vow, saying, "If God will be with me, protect me on this journey, provide food and clothing, and bring me back safely to my father's house, then the Lord will be my God. This stone I have set up will be the house of God, and I will give a tenth of everything You bless me with."

# Chapter XXVIII.

Jacob continued his journey and arrived in the land of the east, at the home of Laban, his mother Rebecca's brother. He stayed there and worked for seven years so he could marry Rachel, Laban's daughter. After completing the seven years, Jacob said to Laban, "I have worked as promised. Now give me Rachel as my wife."

Laban agreed and prepared a wedding feast, but instead of giving Rachel to Jacob, he gave him his older daughter, Leah. He also gave Leah a servant named Zilpah to be her maid. Jacob, unaware of the trick, spent the night with Leah, believing she was Rachel. When he realized the truth, he was furious and said to Laban, "Why have you deceived me? I worked for Rachel, not Leah. This is wrong! Take Leah back and let me go."

Jacob loved Rachel more than Leah. Leah had soft eyes, but Rachel was very beautiful and had a graceful figure. Laban told Jacob, "It is not our custom to marry off the younger daughter before the older one. This rule is also written in the heavenly records—it is a sin to break it." He warned Jacob never to go against this law in the future.

Laban then said, "Finish the wedding celebrations for Leah, and after one week, I will also give you Rachel. But in return, you must work for me another seven years."

Jacob agreed, and after the seven-day celebration for Leah, Laban gave Rachel to him as well. He also gave Rachel a servant named Bilhah to be her maid. Jacob then worked another seven years to fulfill his promise for Rachel.

The Lord saw that Leah was unloved, so He blessed her with children. In the first year of the third week, Leah gave birth to a son and named him Reuben. But Rachel remained childless because the

Lord had not yet given her children, as Jacob loved her more than Leah.

Leah became pregnant again and had a second son, Simeon. Later, she had a third son and named him Levi. Then she gave birth to a fourth son and called him Judah.

Meanwhile, Rachel became jealous of Leah for having children and said to Jacob, "Give me children, or I will die!"

Jacob answered, "I am not God. He alone decides who can have children."

Seeing that Leah had four sons—Reuben, Simeon, Levi, and Judah—Rachel said to Jacob, "Take my servant Bilhah as a wife. She will have children for me."

Rachel gave Bilhah to Jacob, and Bilhah became pregnant and had a son. Rachel named him Dan. Bilhah became pregnant again and had another son, whom Rachel called Naphtali.

Leah noticed that she had stopped having children, so she gave her servant Zilpah to Jacob as a wife. Zilpah gave birth to a son, and Leah named him Gad. Then Zilpah had another son, and Leah named him Asher.

Later, Leah became pregnant again and gave birth to a son named Issachar. She had another son, whom she called Zebulun, and then a daughter, Dinah.

Finally, the Lord answered Rachel's prayers and allowed her to have a child. She became pregnant and gave birth to a son, naming him Joseph.

After Joseph was born, Jacob said to Laban, "Let me take my wives and children and return to my father's house. I have served you faithfully, and now I wish to go home."

Laban replied, "Stay with me a little longer. Name your wages, and I will pay you. Continue caring for my flocks."

They agreed that Jacob's payment would be all the black, spotted, and speckled lambs and goats born among Laban's flocks. Over time, more and more animals were born with these markings, increasing Jacob's share.

Jacob's wealth grew, and he gained many sheep, oxen, camels, donkeys, servants, and maids. However, Laban and his sons became jealous of Jacob's success. Laban started taking back some of the sheep and treated Jacob unfairly.

# Chapter XXIX.

After Rachel gave birth to Joseph, Laban left to shear his sheep, which were three days away from his home. Seeing this as the perfect time to leave, Jacob called Leah and Rachel and spoke to them kindly, asking them to go with him back to the land of Canaan. He told them about a dream in which God instructed him to return to his father's house. Leah and Rachel agreed, saying, "We will go wherever you go."

Jacob then praised the God of his father, Isaac, and his grandfather, Abraham. Early in the morning, he gathered his wives, children, and all his belongings and crossed the river. Without telling Laban, they set out toward Gilead.

In the seventh year of the fourth week, on the twenty-first day of the first month, Jacob began his journey to Gilead. When Laban realized Jacob had left, he chased after him and caught up in the mountains of Gilead on the thirteenth day of the third month. However, God appeared to Laban in a dream that night and warned him not to harm Jacob.

On the fifteenth day, Jacob prepared a feast for Laban and his men. During the gathering, Jacob and Laban made an agreement, promising never to cross the mountains of Gilead with the intent to harm one another. To mark their promise, Jacob built a mound of stones as a witness to their covenant. The place was named "The Heap of Witness."

Before this, the region of Gilead had been home to the Rephaim, a race of giants who were between seven and ten cubits tall. Their land stretched from the territory of the Ammonites to Mount Hermon, including cities like Karnaim, Ashtaroth, Edrei, Misur, and Beon. Because of their wickedness, God wiped them out, and the Amorites later took over their land. No people since have sinned to the same extent as the Rephaim, and their time on earth was cut short.

After making peace, Jacob sent Laban on his way, and Laban returned to Mesopotamia. Jacob continued his journey and crossed the Jabbok River on the eleventh day of the ninth month. That same day, his brother Esau came to meet him. The two brothers reconciled and made peace. Esau then traveled back to the land of Seir, while Jacob remained living in tents.

In the first year of the fifth week, Jacob crossed the Jordan River and settled on the other side. He grazed his flocks from the Sea of the Heap to Bethshan, Dothan, and the Akrabbim forest. From his wealth, Jacob sent gifts to his father Isaac, including clothes, food, meat, drink, milk, butter, cheese, and dates from the valley.

He also sent gifts to his mother Rebecca four times a year—after plowing, during harvest, after autumn, and in the spring. He delivered them to the tower of Abraham, where Rebecca lived.

Meanwhile, Isaac had moved from the Well of the Oath to the tower of Abraham in the mountains of Hebron, living separately from Esau. During Jacob's time in Mesopotamia, Esau married Mahalath,

Ishmael's daughter. Later, Esau moved to Mount Seir with his flocks and wives, leaving Isaac behind at the Well of the Oath. Isaac then relocated to the tower of his father, Abraham.

Jacob continued to provide for his father and mother, sending them whatever they needed. In return, Isaac and Rebecca blessed him with all their hearts and souls.

## Chapter XXX.

In the first year of the sixth week, during the fourth month, Jacob settled in Salem, east of Shechem, arriving safely. While there, Shechem, the son of Hamor the Hivite, the ruler of the land, took Jacob's young daughter Dinah into his house and violated her. She was only twelve years old. Afterward, Shechem wanted to marry Dinah, so he approached his father and then Jacob and his sons with a proposal.

Jacob and his sons were furious about what had been done to Dinah. Although they pretended to respond peacefully, they secretly planned revenge.

Simeon and Levi launched a surprise attack on Shechem, killing all the men in the city to avenge their sister. They left no one alive, making it clear that no daughter of Israel should ever be treated this way again. It was declared in heaven that anyone who committed such a crime deserved to die, for their actions brought disgrace to Israel.

The Lord allowed Jacob's sons to carry out this judgment to prevent others from committing the same sin in the future. It was also commanded that if any Israelite man gave his daughter or sister to a foreigner, he would be put to death by stoning. Likewise, any Israelite woman who dishonored her family by marrying outside of Israel would be burned and removed from the nation.

Israel was called to remain pure before the Lord, avoiding all impurity and unfaithfulness. Anyone who corrupted the nation would face death, as recorded in the heavenly laws. No forgiveness or atonement would be granted to those who violated these laws. Anyone who allowed impurity to spread or gave their children to foreign customs was committing a serious sin and would be cut off from the nation.

Moses was instructed to warn the people of Israel never to marry Gentiles or allow their daughters to do so, for it was considered a terrible offense before the Lord. The story of Shechem was recorded as a warning, showing the judgment carried out by Jacob's sons, who declared, "We will never give our sister to an uncircumcised man, for it would be a disgrace to us."

Marrying outside of Israel was seen as sinful and shameful. Such actions would bring plagues and curses upon the nation. Anyone who ignored this impurity or allowed it to happen would also face judgment and punishment. The entire community would suffer because of it, and the Lord would reject any offerings, sacrifices, or incense from those who committed these sins.

This is why Moses was commanded to teach Israel about the Shechemites and how they were judged by Jacob's sons. Their actions were seen as righteous, and they were written in the heavenly records as a blessing. Levi, in particular, was honored for his dedication to justice. Because of this, he and his descendants were chosen to serve as priests for the Lord forever. His name was recorded in the heavenly tablets as a righteous man and a faithful servant of God.

These events were recorded to remind Israel of their covenant and the importance of following God's laws. If they obeyed, they would be counted as friends of the Lord. But if they sinned and broke the covenant, they would be seen as enemies, erased from the book of life, and placed among those destined for destruction.

On the day Jacob's sons destroyed Shechem, their actions were recorded in heaven as righteous judgment. They rescued Dinah from Shechem's house and took everything from the city—the livestock, goods, and wealth—including sheep, oxen, and donkeys—bringing it all back to Jacob.

Although Jacob was upset with his sons for attacking the city, fearing that the neighboring Canaanites and Perizzites would seek revenge, the fear of the Lord fell upon those nearby. No one dared to attack Jacob's family because terror had spread among the surrounding cities.

# Chapter XXXI.

At the beginning of the month, Jacob gathered his family and said, "Purify yourselves and change into clean clothes. We are going to Bethel, the place where I made a vow to God when I fled from my brother Esau. God has been with me, protected me, and brought me safely back to this land. Now, get rid of any foreign gods among you."

His family handed over their idols, including the ones Rachel had taken from her father Laban, as well as the jewelry they wore in their ears. Jacob collected everything, destroyed them, and buried the remains under an oak tree in Shechem.

Jacob then traveled to Bethel at the beginning of the seventh month. He built an altar at the place where he had once slept and set up a pillar in honor of the Lord. He sent a message to his father, Isaac, inviting him and his mother, Rebekah, to join him for the sacrifice. Isaac replied, "Let my son Jacob come to me so I may see him before I die."

Jacob brought his sons, Levi and Judah, to visit Isaac. When Rebekah heard that Jacob had arrived, she left the tower and ran to meet him. Her heart filled with joy when she heard, "Jacob, your son, has returned." She embraced him tightly, kissed him, and wept with happiness. Then she saw Levi and Judah and asked, "Are these your sons, my child?" She hugged and kissed them, blessing them, and said, "Through you, the descendants of Abraham will become a great people, bringing blessings to the world."

Jacob entered Isaac's room, where his father lay resting. He took Isaac's hand, leaned down, and kissed him. Isaac held Jacob close and wept. Though his eyesight was failing, his spirit lifted, and he asked, "Are these your sons? They look just like you." Jacob confirmed that they were.

Isaac kissed both boys, and suddenly, the spirit of prophecy filled him. He took Levi's right hand and Judah's left, then began to bless Levi first.

"May the eternal God bless you and your children. May you be chosen and set apart to serve in His holy place, just like the angels in heaven. Your family will be honored and respected, always serving in God's presence. Your descendants will lead and guide the tribes of Israel, teaching them His laws and commandments. His blessings will be spoken through you, and you will bring goodness to all His people."

Isaac continued, "Your mother named you Levi, and your name is fitting because you will always be connected to the Lord. You will share in the inheritance with Jacob's sons, and your family will receive blessings from God's table. May you never be in need and always have more than enough. Anyone who stands against you will fail, and those who curse you will be cursed, but those who bless you will be blessed."

Then Isaac turned to Judah and said, "May the Lord give you the strength to defeat your enemies. You will be a leader among your brothers, and from your family will come a ruler who will govern the descendants of Jacob. Your name will be known everywhere, and nations will respect your family. Through you, Jacob's people will find help, and Israel will be saved. When you rule with fairness, peace will spread to all of God's people. Those who bless you will be blessed, and those who stand against you will fade away."

Isaac kissed Judah, hugged him, and felt great joy at seeing Jacob's sons. He blessed them once more and then rested at Jacob's feet. That evening, Isaac and Jacob ate together, celebrating with happiness. Jacob placed Levi and Judah on either side of Isaac as they slept, and Isaac felt it was a righteous act.

That night, Jacob shared stories with Isaac about how the Lord had been with him, protected him, and blessed him. Isaac praised the God of Abraham for showing mercy to Jacob and his family.

The next morning, Jacob told Isaac about the vow he had made at Bethel, describing the vision he had seen and the altar he had built. Isaac said, "I am too old to travel, my son. I am 165 years old and no longer strong enough to make the journey. Take your mother with you and fulfill the vow you made to the Lord without delay. Be faithful to it, for you are responsible for keeping your promise. May the Creator of all things accept your offering and be pleased."

Isaac instructed Rebekah to go with Jacob, and she traveled with him, bringing her servant Deborah. As they made their way to Bethel, Jacob reflected on Isaac's blessings over Levi and Judah, and his heart was filled with gratitude. He praised the God of his fathers, Abraham and Isaac, saying, "Now I know that my future is secure, and that my sons will also be blessed before the Lord forever."

This moment was recorded in the heavenly books as an eternal testimony of Isaac's blessings over Levi and Judah.

# Chapter XXXII.

That night, Jacob stayed in Bethel, and Levi had a dream where God chose him and his descendants to serve as priests for the Most High forever. When he woke up, Levi praised and thanked God for this great honor.

The next morning, on the fourteenth day of the month, Jacob dedicated a tenth of everything he owned—his servants, livestock, gold, silver, and all his possessions—as an offering to God. Around this time, Rachel became pregnant with her son, Benjamin. Jacob counted his sons and decided that Levi's share would be set apart for the Lord. He dressed Levi in priestly robes and gave him the responsibility of serving as a priest.

On the fifteenth day of the month, Jacob made a sacrifice at the altar, offering fourteen oxen, twenty-eight rams, forty-nine sheep, seven lambs, and twenty-one goats, along with grain and drink offerings. This was to fulfill a promise he had made to God. After the fire consumed the sacrifices, Jacob burned incense on the altar as an offering of thanksgiving.

For the next seven days, he continued making offerings, sacrificing two oxen, four rams, four sheep, four goats, and two lambs each day. Jacob, his sons, and his household celebrated with food and drink, thanking God for His kindness and protection.

Jacob also offered a tenth of all his clean animals as a burnt offering to the Lord. However, the unclean animals were not included in Levi's portion. Levi served as a priest at Bethel, leading the offerings before Jacob and his brothers. Jacob renewed his promise to God, dedicating another tithe and setting it apart for the Lord. This became a lasting tradition: every year, the second tithe was to be eaten in the place God chose, with none of it left over. Any tithe not eaten by the end of the year would be considered unclean and burned.

Jacob then planned to build a sacred place at Bethel, enclosing it with a wall to create a permanent sanctuary for himself and his descendants. That night, the Lord appeared to him, blessed him, and said, "Your name will no longer be Jacob but Israel." God promised that Jacob's family would grow into many nations and that kings would come from his descendants. He also reaffirmed that the land under heaven would belong to Jacob's children, who would rule over many nations.

After God finished speaking, Jacob watched as He ascended into heaven. Later that night, Jacob had another dream where an angel came down from heaven carrying seven tablets. The angel handed them to Jacob, and as he read them, he understood everything that would happen to him and his descendants in the future.

The angel told Jacob not to build a permanent sanctuary at Bethel but to return to his father's house until Isaac passed away. The angel also revealed that Jacob would die peacefully in Egypt and be buried with honor alongside Abraham and Isaac.

The angel reassured Jacob not to be afraid, promising that everything he had seen and read would come true. When Jacob worried about remembering all the details, the angel told him that he would recall them when the time was right.

After the vision ended, Jacob woke up, remembering everything he had seen. He wrote it all down and, the next day, made another offering as he had before. He named the day "Addition" because it was added to the yearly feast days, and it became a part of Israel's yearly celebrations.

On the night of the twenty-third of the month, Deborah, Rebekah's nurse, passed away. Jacob buried her near a river by the city, under an oak tree, naming the place "The River of Deborah" and the tree "The Oak of Deborah's Mourning."

Rebekah returned home with Isaac, and Jacob sent gifts of rams, sheep, and goats for them to prepare a meal. Later, Jacob traveled to the land of Kabratan to be near his mother and stayed there for a while.

During this time, Rachel gave birth to a son. Her labor was very painful, and she named him "Son of My Sorrow." However, Jacob changed his name to Benjamin. Sadly, Rachel died during childbirth, and Jacob buried her in Ephrath, which is also called Bethlehem. He set up a pillar on her grave as a marker, and it remained there along the road.

# Chapter XXXIII.

Jacob settled with his wife Leah south of Magdaladra'ef on the first day of the tenth month. Around this time, Reuben, Jacob's oldest son, saw Bilhah, Rachel's servant and his father's concubine, bathing in a private place. He was attracted to her and waited until nighttime to act on his desires.

Late at night, Reuben secretly entered Bilhah's tent while she was sleeping alone. He lay with her, and when she woke up and realized what had happened, she was horrified. Bilhah screamed when she recognized Reuben and clung to her blanket in shame. Reuben ran away, leaving her deeply distressed. She was overcome with grief but kept what had happened to herself.

When Jacob returned to Bilhah, she told him everything, saying, "I am no longer pure for you because I have been dishonored. Reuben lay with me while I was asleep, and I didn't know until he uncovered my blanket and defiled me." Jacob was furious with Reuben for committing such a terrible sin, bringing shame upon his father. From that day forward, Jacob never went to Bilhah again.

This act was a great sin in God's eyes. It is strictly forbidden for a man to be with his father's wife or bring shame upon his father in this way. Such behavior is disgraceful and offensive to the Lord. It is written in the heavenly records that no man should ever commit this sin. The punishment for it is death by stoning, and both the man and the woman involved must be removed from the people of God to keep the nation pure.

It is also written, "Cursed is the man who lies with his father's wife, for he has shamed his father." And all the holy ones of the Lord declared, "Amen." Moses was commanded to teach this law to the children of Israel, for it carries the penalty of death. It is a serious impurity, and there is no forgiveness for it. Anyone who commits this sin must be put to death immediately and removed from the community. Such a person must not remain alive even for a single day, as their actions have polluted the people of God.

Although Reuben was not punished while Jacob was alive, it was only because the full law and its judgment had not yet been given. Now, this law is established forever for all generations. There is no atonement for this sin. Anyone who commits it must be removed from the nation and put to death on the same day. Moses was commanded to write down this law so that Israel would follow it and avoid sins that lead to destruction.

The Lord, who is a just Judge, does not show favoritism and cannot be bribed. Moses was to remind the people of this covenant so they would obey it and protect themselves from being cut off from the land. Anyone who commits this sin is considered unclean before God. There is no greater impurity on earth than this kind of wrongdoing. Israel is a holy nation, chosen by God to receive His promises—a people set apart to serve Him. Such impurity must not be found among them.

In the third year of the sixth week, Jacob and all his sons moved to the home of Abraham, near Isaac, his father, and Rebekah, his mother. Jacob's sons were: Reuben, the firstborn; Simeon, Levi, Judah, Issachar, and Zebulun, the sons of Leah; Joseph and Benjamin, the sons of Rachel; Dan and Naphtali, the sons of Bilhah; Gad and Asher, the sons of Zilpah; and Dinah, Leah's only daughter.

When they arrived, they bowed in respect before Isaac and Rebekah, and Isaac blessed Jacob and his sons. Seeing Jacob's children filled Isaac with joy. He spoke blessings over them, praising God for the family that had grown through Jacob.

## Chapter XXXIV.

In the sixth year of the forty-fourth jubilee, Jacob sent his sons and their servants to graze the sheep near Shechem. While they were there, seven kings of the Amorites made a plan to attack them. They hid among the trees, waiting for the right moment to steal their livestock.

At that time, Jacob was at home with Levi, Judah, Joseph, and Isaac because Isaac was feeling sorrowful, and they didn't want to leave him alone. Benjamin, the youngest, also stayed with his father.

The kings of Taphu, Aresa, Seragan, Selo, Ga'as, Bethoron, and Ma'anisakir, who were from Canaan, learned about the Amorites' plot and sent a message to Jacob: "The Amorite kings have surrounded your sons and taken their herds."

Jacob immediately gathered Levi, Judah, Joseph, his father's servants, and his own men, making a total of six thousand warriors armed with swords. They marched to Shechem to face the Amorites. A fierce battle broke out, and Jacob's forces chased down and defeated the Amorites. They killed the kings of Aresa, Taphu, Seragan, Selo, Ga'as, and Ma'anisakir, reclaimed the stolen livestock, and subdued their enemies.

After the battle, Jacob forced the defeated kings to pay tribute by giving five types of fruit from their land. He also built two cities, Robel and Tamnatares, before returning home safely. The defeated kings remained under Jacob's rule until he and his sons later moved to Egypt.

In the seventh year of the next week, Jacob sent Joseph to check on his brothers in Shechem. However, Joseph found them in Dothan, where they had moved their flocks. When Joseph arrived, his brothers plotted against him, intending to kill him. But instead of going through with their plan, they decided to sell him to Ishmaelite merchants. These merchants took Joseph to Egypt and sold him to Potiphar, Pharaoh's chief cook and a priest in the city of 'Elew.

To cover up their actions, Joseph's brothers killed a goat, dipped his coat in its blood, and sent it to Jacob on the tenth day of the seventh month. When Jacob saw the blood-stained coat, he believed that a wild animal had killed Joseph. Overcome with sorrow, he cried, "A wild beast has devoured Joseph!" His entire household mourned with him that day, but Jacob refused to be comforted, saying, "I will grieve for my son until I go to my grave."

That same month, Bilhah, who was living in Qafratef, was so heartbroken after hearing about Joseph's death that she passed away. Soon after, Dinah, Jacob's daughter, also died. Within a single month,

Jacob lost Bilhah, Dinah, and Joseph—or so he believed. Both Bilhah and Dinah were buried near Rachel's grave.

Jacob mourned for Joseph for an entire year and could not find peace. Again and again, he repeated, "I will go to my grave mourning for my son."

Later, it was commanded that the people of Israel fast on the tenth day of the seventh month—the day Jacob learned of Joseph's supposed death. This was to be a day of atonement for their sins, marked by the sacrifice of a young goat. It also served as a reminder of the deep sorrow Jacob felt for Joseph and was set as a time for spiritual cleansing.

After Joseph was gone, Jacob's sons began to marry.

- Reuben married Ada.
- Simeon first married Adlba'a, a Canaanite, but later repented and married another wife from Mesopotamia, following the example of his brothers.
- Levi married Melka, a daughter of Aram from Terah's family.
- Judah married Betasu'el, a Canaanite.
- Issachar married Hezaqa.
- Zebulun married Ni'iman.
- Dan married Egla.
- Naphtali married Rasu'u from Mesopotamia.
- Gad married Maka.
- Asher married Ijona.
- Joseph later married Asenath, an Egyptian.
- Benjamin married Ijasaka.

# Chapter XXXV.

In the first year of the first week of the forty-fifth jubilee, Rebecca called Jacob to her and gave him advice about his father and brother. She told him to always respect and care for them.

Jacob replied, "I will do everything you ask, Mother. Treating them with respect will bring me blessings and favor from God. You know my heart and how I have lived my life. I have always tried to do what is right for others. How could I not honor my father and brother as you want? If I have done anything wrong, please tell me, and I will correct it so that God will have mercy on me."

Rebecca said, "My son, I have never seen you do anything wrong, only good. But I must tell you something important. My time is near, and I will die this year. I will not live beyond the age of 155. I have seen it in a dream, and I know it is true."

Jacob laughed at her words because Rebecca was still strong and healthy. She had no sign of illness, moved around easily, and had never been sick. Jacob said, "Mother, if I could live as long as you and still be as strong as you are, I would consider it a blessing. You won't die; you must be joking with me."

Rebecca then went to Isaac and said, "I have a request, my husband. Please make Esau promise that he will not harm Jacob or stay angry with him. You know how Esau has always been—he has been difficult since childhood, and there is no kindness in him. After you pass away, he plans to kill Jacob. You have seen how he has treated us, especially after Jacob left for Haran. He took your flocks and stole from us, and when we asked for what was rightfully ours, he acted like he was doing us a favor. He is still upset because you blessed Jacob, who is honest and righteous. But since Jacob came back, he has cared for us in every way. He shares what he has, respects us, and treats us with kindness."

Isaac replied, "I know everything Jacob has done. He honors us with all his heart. I used to love Esau more because he was my firstborn, but now I love Jacob more because Esau has chosen a sinful path. He does not follow what is right; he has become violent and corrupt. He has turned away from the God of Abraham and follows the ways of his wives, who have led him into impurity. Neither he nor his descendants will be saved; they will be destroyed. As for making Esau promise, even if he does, he will not keep his word. But do not worry about Jacob. He is protected by Someone far greater than Esau's strength."

Rebecca then called Esau to her. When he arrived, she said, "I have a request, my son. Will you promise to do what I ask?"

Esau answered, "I will do whatever you ask, Mother. I will not refuse you."

Rebecca said, "When I die, bury me near Sarah, your father's mother. Also, love your brother Jacob and do not harm him. If you and Jacob love each other, you will both prosper and be honored in this land. No enemy will have power over you, and you will be a blessing to those who love you."

Esau promised, "I will do everything you ask. I will bury you near Sarah when you pass, and I will love Jacob. He is my brother, and it is only natural to love him—we are family. If I do not love him, who else should I love? I also ask that you speak to Jacob about me and my sons. I know he will rule over us, for when my father blessed him, he made him greater and me lesser."

Esau swore to Rebecca that he would do as she asked. Then Rebecca called Jacob to stand before Esau and gave him the same instructions. Jacob replied, "I will do everything you ask. I promise that neither I nor my sons will ever harm Esau. I will only love him."

That evening, they shared a meal and drank together. That night, Rebecca passed away at the age of 155. Esau and Jacob buried her in the cave near Sarah, their grandmother.

# Chapter XXXVI.

In the sixth year of that time, Isaac called his two sons, Esau and Jacob, to come to him. He said, "My sons, my time is near. I will soon go to be with our ancestors. When I pass, bury me next to my father Abraham in the cave in the field of Ephron the Hittite—the same tomb Abraham bought for our family. That is where I have prepared my resting place.

I ask you, my sons, to live with honesty and fairness, so that the Lord will fulfill the promises He made to Abraham and his descendants. Love one another as you love your own life. Support each other, work together, and let your bond be strong.

I warn you not to worship idols or be drawn to them. They mislead those who follow them. Remember the Lord, the God of Abraham, and how I served Him with joy and faithfulness. Because of this, He blessed me, made my descendants as numerous as the stars, and established us as a righteous people who will last forever.

Now, I will have you swear a great oath—by the name of the One who created everything in heaven and on earth—that you will honor and worship Him alone. Love your brother with honesty and goodness, and never plan harm against him. If you do this, you will be successful in everything, and no harm will come to you.

But if one of you plots evil against his brother, that person will bring destruction upon himself. He will be cut off from the land of the living, and his family will not survive. When God's wrath comes, as it did in Sodom, his land, city, and everything he owns will be destroyed.

His name will be erased from the book of the righteous and placed among those who are condemned. He will face suffering and sorrow forever.

I warn you, my sons: anyone who harms his brother will face judgment. Today, I am dividing my belongings between you. Since Esau is the firstborn, he will receive the larger portion, including the tower and everything Abraham owned at the Well of the Oath."

Esau replied, "I already sold my birthright to Jacob. It belongs to him, and I have no claim to it."

Isaac said, "May God's blessing rest on both of you and your descendants from this day forward. You have brought me peace by making things right between you. My heart is no longer troubled about the birthright. May the Most High bless those who act with righteousness and extend that blessing to their children forever."

After blessing them, Isaac gave his final instructions. They ate and drank together in his presence, and Isaac was filled with joy, knowing his sons were at peace. That night, they went to rest, and Isaac lay in his bed, content. Soon after, he passed away peacefully. He lived to be 180 years old, completing twenty-five weeks and five years. His sons, Esau and Jacob, buried him.

Esau moved to the land of Edom and settled in the mountains of Seir. Jacob remained in the mountains of Hebron, living in the same tower where his grandfather Abraham had once stayed. He continued to worship the Lord with all his heart, following the commands that had been passed down through his family.

In the fourth year of the second week of the forty-fifth jubilee, Jacob's wife Leah passed away. He buried her in the same cave where his mother, Rebecca, had been laid, to the left of Sarah, the mother of his father. All her sons, along with Jacob's other children, came together to mourn her and to comfort Jacob, for he loved her deeply after Rachel had died.

Leah had been kind, faithful, and righteous all her life. She always honored Jacob and never spoke harshly to him. She was gentle, loving, and respectable. Jacob remembered her goodness and mourned her loss with all his heart and soul.

# Chapter XXXVII.

On the day Isaac, the father of Jacob and Esau, passed away, Esau's sons found out that Isaac had given the birthright to Jacob, even though Esau was the older son. They were furious and demanded answers from their father.

"Why did your father give the firstborn's blessing to Jacob instead of you?" they asked.

Esau answered, "I sold my birthright to Jacob for a bowl of lentils. Later, when our father sent me to hunt and bring him food so he could bless me, Jacob tricked me. He brought food to our father first and received the blessing that was meant for me. After that, our father made us both swear to live in peace, to love each other, and not to harm one another."

But Esau's sons refused to listen. "We will not make peace with Jacob," they declared. "We are stronger than he is. We will fight him, kill him, and wipe out his sons. And if you refuse to help us, we will deal with you too."

They continued, "Let's send messengers to Aram, Philistia, Moab, and Ammon to gather warriors who love to fight. With their help, we will destroy Jacob before he grows even more powerful."

Esau tried to stop them. "Do not go to war with him," he warned. "If you do, you may be the ones who fall."

But his sons ignored him. "You have spent your whole life obeying Jacob. We will not follow your advice."

Determined to carry out their plan, they sent messengers to Esau's ally, Aduram, and hired a thousand warriors. They also gathered a thousand fighters each from Moab, Ammon, Philistia, Edom, and the Horites. From the Kittim, they brought mighty warriors. Then, turning to Esau, they threatened, "Lead us into battle, or we will kill you."

Filled with anger and frustration, Esau finally agreed. As old feelings of resentment returned, he forgot the oath he had sworn to his parents and allowed his heart to turn against Jacob once again.

Meanwhile, Jacob had no idea that trouble was coming. He was still mourning the death of Leah, his wife, when Esau and his army of four thousand warriors came near the tower where he was staying. The people of Hebron, who respected Jacob more than Esau because of his kindness and generosity, rushed to warn him.

"Esau is coming with four thousand armed men, ready for battle," they told him.

At first, Jacob didn't believe them. But when he saw the army approaching, he quickly shut the gates of the tower and climbed to the top. From there, he called out to Esau.

"Is this how you come to comfort me after my wife's death? Is this how you keep the oath you swore to our father and mother? You have broken your promise and brought judgment upon yourself."

Esau replied bitterly, "Oaths mean nothing. People and animals alike will always fight their enemies. You have hated me and my children for as long as I can remember. We are not brothers, and we never will be."

Then Esau spoke in anger:

"If a wild boar could grow soft fur like a lamb,
    If it could sprout horns like a ram or a deer,
    Then I would make peace with you.

If a mother could leave her newborn child,
    Then I would call you my brother.

If wolves could lie down with lambs,
    Without trying to tear them apart,
    And their hearts became kind,
    Then I would make peace with you.

If a lion and an ox could work together,
    Plowing the fields side by side,
    Then I would make peace with you.

If a raven could turn as white as snow,
    Then you would know that I loved you.

But you and your children will be torn from the land,
    And there will never be peace for you.

When Jacob saw the hatred in Esau's heart and the fury in his eyes, he realized Esau was determined to destroy him. Understanding that words would not change his brother's mind, he compared Esau to a wild boar charging straight into a spear.

Jacob then turned to his men and said, "Prepare your weapons. Stand ready. We will not run from this fight."

# Chapter XXXVIII.

After that, Judah turned to his father, Jacob, and said, "Father, take your bow and shoot your arrows to defend us. Show your strength, but do not let us harm your brother. He is still your own flesh and blood and should face you in this battle."

Jacob took his bow and fired an arrow, hitting Esau on the right side of his chest, killing him instantly. He shot another arrow, striking 'Adoran the Aramean on his left side, knocking him backward and killing him as well.

Then, Jacob's sons and their servants split into groups and attacked the enemy from all directions around the tower. Judah led the southern group with Naphtali, Gad, and fifty servants. Together, they fought fiercely, leaving no survivors. On the eastern side, Levi, Dan, and Asher, along with fifty men, faced the warriors from Moab and Ammon, defeating them all. Reuben, Issachar, and Zebulon took the north side with fifty men and overpowered the fighters from Philistia. Meanwhile, Simeon, Benjamin, and Enoch, Reuben's son, attacked from the west with fifty men, defeating four hundred warriors from Edom and the Horites.

Even though six hundred men, including four of Esau's sons, managed to escape, they left Esau's body behind on the hill of 'Aduram. Jacob buried Esau there and returned home.

Jacob's sons pursued Esau's fleeing sons into the mountains of Seir, where they captured them and made them serve Jacob's descendants. They sent word to Jacob, asking if they should make peace with Esau's sons or destroy them completely. Jacob instructed them to make peace, so they did, placing Esau's descendants under their rule and requiring them to pay tribute to Jacob and his sons for generations.

Esau's descendants continued to pay tribute until the day Jacob and his family moved to Egypt. Even today, the people of Edom remain under the rule of Jacob's descendants and have never been able to free themselves from this obligation.

These are the kings who ruled over Edom before Israel had any kings:

- The first king was Balaq, son of Beor, and his city was called Danaba.
- After Balaq died, Jobab, son of Zara from Boser, became king.
- When Jobab died, 'Asam from the land of Teman took the throne.
- After 'Asam's death, 'Adath, son of Barad—who had defeated the Midianites in the field of Moab—became king. His city was called Avith.
- When 'Adath died, Salman from 'Amaseqa ruled as king.
- After Salman, Saul from Ra'aboth by the river took the throne.
- Saul was followed by Ba'elunan, son of Achbor.
- When Ba'elunan died, 'Adath became king again, and his wife was Maitabith, daughter of Matarat, granddaughter of Metabedza'ab.

These kings ruled over Edom before any king was established in Israel.

# Chapter XXXIX.

Jacob stayed in the land of Canaan, where his father had once lived. These are the events of his family's story.

Joseph, at seventeen years old, was taken to Egypt and sold to Potiphar, a high-ranking officer of Pharaoh and the captain of the guard. Potiphar put Joseph in charge of his entire household, and because of Joseph, the Lord blessed everything in Potiphar's home. Everything Joseph did was successful, and Potiphar noticed that God was with him, making him prosper in all he did. Because of this, Potiphar gave Joseph complete authority over everything he owned.

Joseph was strong and handsome, which caught the attention of Potiphar's wife. She became obsessed with him and constantly asked him to be with her. But Joseph refused. He remembered what his father, Jacob, had taught him about the words of Abraham: that committing adultery with a married woman was a terrible sin, deserving of death according to God's laws. Joseph held on to these teachings and refused to betray his master or sin against God.

For an entire year, Potiphar's wife tried to convince Joseph, but he resisted. One day, when they were alone, she grabbed his coat and tried to force him to be with her. Joseph pulled away, leaving his coat in her hands, and ran out of the house. Furious at being rejected, she decided to take revenge. She screamed and told the household servants that Joseph had attacked her. Later, when her husband came home, she said, "That Hebrew slave you trust tried to take advantage of me. When I screamed, he ran away, leaving his coat behind."

Hearing this, Potiphar became angry. Seeing the coat as proof, he had Joseph thrown into prison, where the king's prisoners were kept. But even in prison, the Lord was with Joseph. The chief jailer noticed how responsible and successful Joseph was in everything he did. Recognizing that God was with him, the jailer put Joseph in charge of all the prisoners, trusting him completely to manage everything well.

Joseph remained in prison for two years. During that time, Pharaoh became angry with two of his officials—the chief cupbearer and the chief baker—and had them imprisoned in the same place as Joseph.

The jailer assigned Joseph to take care of them.

One night, both the cupbearer and the baker had dreams that troubled them. They shared their dreams with Joseph, and with God's help, he explained their meanings. Just as Joseph predicted, the cupbearer was restored to his position, while the baker was executed.

Before the cupbearer was released, Joseph asked him to remember him and mention his situation to Pharaoh, hoping to be freed. However, once the cupbearer returned to his position, he completely forgot about Joseph and did not speak of him to Pharaoh. Despite Joseph's kindness, the cupbearer did not remember him at all.

## Chapter XL.

One night, Pharaoh had two dreams about a great famine that was coming to the land. When he woke up, he called all the dream interpreters and magicians in Egypt to explain his dreams. But none of them could understand what they meant. Then, the chief butler remembered Joseph and told Pharaoh about him. Joseph was taken out of prison and brought before Pharaoh to hear the dreams.

Joseph told Pharaoh, "Both of your dreams mean the same thing. There will be seven years of great harvests, with plenty of food across Egypt. But after that, seven years of famine will come, so severe that people will forget the years of plenty."

He then advised Pharaoh, "You should put wise and responsible men in charge of storing extra food in every city during the seven good years. That way, when the famine comes, there will be enough food to keep people alive, and Egypt will not be ruined by hunger."

God gave Joseph wisdom and favor in Pharaoh's eyes. Pharaoh said to his servants, "There is no one as wise as Joseph. The spirit of

God is with him." So Pharaoh made Joseph the second most powerful man in all of Egypt. He gave Joseph control over the entire land and had him ride in his second chariot. He dressed Joseph in fine clothes, placed a gold chain around his neck, and gave him his official ring as a sign of his authority. A messenger went before him, announcing his new position. Pharaoh told Joseph, "Only I, as king, will be greater than you."

Joseph ruled fairly over Egypt. The officials and workers respected him, and he treated everyone with honesty. He never took bribes or showed favoritism. Because of him, Egypt was peaceful, and God continued to bless him. People admired Joseph, and Pharaoh's kingdom remained well-run and free from trouble.

Pharaoh gave Joseph a new name, Zaphenath-Paneah, and arranged his marriage to Asenath, the daughter of Potipherah, a priest from On. Joseph was thirty years old when he stood before Pharaoh. That same year, Isaac passed away. Just as Joseph had predicted, the land had seven years of plenty. The harvests were so abundant that one portion of seed produced eighteen hundred times more. Joseph collected and stored food in every city until the grain supply was so large that it couldn't even be measured.

# Chapter XLI.

During the forty-fifth jubilee, in the second week of the second year, Judah arranged for his oldest son, Er, to marry a woman named Tamar, who came from the daughters of Aram. However, Er did not love her because she wasn't from his mother's Canaanite family. He wanted to marry someone from his mother's people, but Judah refused to allow it. Er was wicked in God's eyes, so God took his life.

After Er's death, Judah told his second son, Onan, to marry Tamar and have children on behalf of his late brother. But Onan knew the children wouldn't be considered his, so he purposely avoided making her pregnant. This angered God, and Onan also died.

Judah then told Tamar to stay in her father's house as a widow until his youngest son, Shelah, was old enough to marry her. However, when Shelah grew up, Judah's wife, Bedsu'el, was against the marriage. In the fifth year of that week, Bedsu'el passed away. The next year, Judah went to Timnah to shear his sheep.

When Tamar heard that Judah was going to Timnah, she took off her widow's clothing, covered her face with a veil, and dressed beautifully. She waited by the road where Judah would pass. When Judah saw her, he thought she was a prostitute and approached her. He said, "Let me be with you." Tamar asked, "What will you give me in return?" Judah replied, "I don't have anything with me right now, but I will leave my signet ring, necklace, and staff as a guarantee until I send payment." Tamar agreed, and they were together. As a result, she became pregnant.

Afterward, Tamar returned home. Later, Judah sent a servant with a young goat to pay her and get his items back, but the servant couldn't find her. The locals told him, "There has been no prostitute here." When the servant returned and told Judah, he said, "Let her keep the items. We don't want to be embarrassed."

Three months later, Judah was told, "Tamar, your daughter-in-law, is pregnant from prostitution." Enraged, Judah went to her father's house and demanded that she be burned as punishment. As she was being taken out, Tamar sent a message to Judah, saying, "The man who owns these items is the father of my child. Do you recognize them?" She showed the signet ring, necklace, and staff. Judah immediately knew they were his and admitted, "She is more righteous than I am. I failed to give her to my son Shelah, as I promised." Judah stopped the punishment, and Tamar's life was spared.

Tamar was never married to Shelah, and Judah never had relations with her again. Later, she gave birth to twin boys, Perez and Zerah, in the seventh year of the second week. Around this time, the seven years of abundance that Joseph had predicted for Egypt came to an end.

Judah deeply regretted what he had done. He realized his mistake and sincerely repented before God. Because of his honest confession, God forgave him, and he never repeated the sin. In a dream, he was assured that his wrongdoing had been forgiven because he had shown true remorse and made amends.

It was also revealed to him that his other sons were not responsible for what had happened with Tamar, and because of this, his family line continued. Judah had followed the strict traditions passed down from Abraham when he first sought to punish Tamar, and his actions later influenced the laws that were established.

# Chapter XLII.

In the first year of the third week of the forty-fifth jubilee, a terrible famine spread across the land. The rains stopped, and the ground became dry and lifeless. But in Egypt, there was still food because Joseph had wisely stored grain during the seven good years. As the famine worsened, the Egyptians came to Joseph to buy food, and he opened the storehouses, selling grain in exchange for gold.

Meanwhile, Canaan was struggling. When Jacob heard there was food in Egypt, he sent ten of his sons to buy grain, but he did not let Benjamin go with them. When the brothers arrived in Egypt along with other people looking for food, Joseph recognized them immediately, but they did not know who he was. Acting like a stranger, Joseph accused them of being spies. "Are you here to find weaknesses in our land?" he asked. He then put them in prison for a few days. Later, he released nine of them but kept Simeon as a hostage, telling them to return with their youngest brother to prove they were telling the truth. Without them knowing, Joseph secretly filled their sacks with grain and returned their money.

Back in Canaan, the brothers told Jacob everything that had happened. They explained how the ruler of Egypt accused them of spying and would not release Simeon unless they brought Benjamin back. Jacob was heartbroken. "You have already taken my children from me! Joseph is gone, Simeon is gone, and now you want to take Benjamin too? Everything is against me!" he cried. He refused to let Benjamin go. "His mother had only two sons. One is already gone. If something happens to him, I will be in sorrow for the rest of my life."

When they found their money inside their sacks, they became even more afraid, and Jacob refused to send Benjamin with them. But the famine only grew worse, while Egypt still had plenty of food because of Joseph's careful planning. As their supplies ran low, Jacob told his sons, "Go back and buy more food, or we will starve." But they replied, "We cannot go back unless Benjamin is with us. The man was clear— we must bring him."

Seeing no other choice, Jacob finally agreed. Reuben offered, "Trust him to me. If I don't bring him back, you can take my two sons." But Jacob refused. Then Judah stepped forward and said, "Send him with me. I will take full responsibility. If I don't bring him back, I will carry the blame forever."

At last, Jacob agreed and sent Benjamin with them. He also told them to bring gifts for the Egyptian leader: stacte, almonds, terebinth nuts, and pure honey. On the first day of the second year of the famine, they left for Egypt.

When they arrived, Joseph immediately recognized Benjamin but did not reveal who he was. "Is this your youngest brother?" he asked. "Yes," they answered. Joseph then said, "May the Lord be gracious to you, my son."

Joseph invited them to his house, released Simeon, and prepared a feast. The brothers gave him the gifts, and they all ate and drank together. During the meal, Joseph gave food to each of them, but he gave Benjamin seven times more than the others.

Before they left, Joseph wanted to test them. He told his servant, "Fill their sacks with grain, return their money, and put my silver cup— the one I drink from—in the youngest brother's sack. Then send them on their way."

## Chapter XLIII.

The steward followed Joseph's instructions exactly. He filled the brothers' sacks with food, returned their money, and secretly placed Joseph's silver cup in Benjamin's sack. Early the next morning, the brothers left for home. But soon after, Joseph told his steward, "Go after them. When you catch them, ask, 'Why have you repaid kindness with betrayal? You stole my master's special cup!' Bring the youngest back to me right away—I must decide what to do with him."

The steward chased after them, caught up, and repeated Joseph's words. The brothers were shocked and said, "Why would you accuse us of this? We would never steal from your master! We even brought back the money we found in our sacks last time. Why would we take silver from his house? Search our bags! If you find the cup with anyone, let him die, and the rest of us will become your slaves."

The steward replied, "No, only the one who has the cup will stay as my servant. The rest of you may go free."

He searched their sacks, starting with the oldest and ending with the youngest. When he opened Benjamin's sack, there was the silver cup. The brothers were devastated. They tore their clothes in grief, loaded their donkeys, and returned to the city.

When they reached Joseph's house, they fell to the ground before him. Joseph asked, "What have you done? Didn't you think I would find out the truth?"

The brothers answered, "What can we say? How can we prove our innocence? God has exposed our guilt. We are your servants now, including the one who had the cup."

Joseph responded, "I fear God. I will not punish all of you. Only the one who stole the cup will stay as my servant. The rest of you may return to your father."

At this, Judah stepped forward and pleaded, "My lord, please listen. We have an elderly father who loves his youngest son dearly. His life is tied to this boy. If we return without him, our father will die of heartbreak. Please let me stay as your servant instead, and let the boy go home with his brothers. I promised my father I would bring him back safely. If I fail, I will carry this guilt forever."

Joseph could no longer hold back his emotions. Seeing their love for one another, he ordered everyone else to leave the room. Then, with tears streaming down his face, he said in Hebrew, "I am Joseph, your brother."

The brothers were too shocked to speak. Joseph continued, "It's really me—the one you sold into Egypt. But don't be afraid or blame yourselves. God sent me here ahead of you to save lives. This famine has already lasted two years, and there are still five more years without harvests or food. God used me to ensure survival. Hurry back to our father and tell him I'm alive and that God has made me ruler of all Egypt. Bring him and your families here so I can take care of you during the remaining years of famine."

Joseph hugged each of his brothers, crying with them. Then he provided them with wagons, supplies for their journey, fine clothes, and silver. For his father, he sent ten donkeys loaded with the best goods from Egypt, along with grain and bread for the trip.

When the brothers returned to Canaan, they told their father, "Joseph is alive! He is the ruler of all Egypt!" Jacob was stunned and couldn't believe it at first. But when he saw the wagons and all the provisions Joseph had sent, his spirit was lifted. He said, "That is enough! My son Joseph is alive! I will go and see him before I die."

# Chapter XLIV.

Israel left Haran on the first day of the third month, beginning his journey to Egypt. On the seventh day, he reached the Well of the Oath and offered a sacrifice to the God of his father, Isaac. As he remembered the dream he had at Bethel, he felt unsure and afraid to continue to Egypt. He thought about sending for Joseph instead, so he wouldn't have to leave Canaan. He stayed there for seven days, seeking guidance and hoping for a sign. During this time, he observed the festival of the first-fruits, even though there was no grain to plant because of the severe famine, which had affected crops, animals, birds, and people alike.

On the sixteenth day of the month, the Lord appeared to Jacob in a vision and called, "Jacob, Jacob." Jacob answered, "Here I am." The Lord said, "I am the God of your fathers, the God of Abraham and

Isaac. Do not be afraid to go to Egypt. I will make your family into a great nation there. I will be with you and bring you back safely. You will be buried in your homeland, and Joseph will be with you when you die. Have no fear—go to Egypt."

Encouraged by this, Jacob gathered his sons, grandsons, and belongings. They placed him and all they owned on wagons, and on the sixteenth day of the third month, they left the Well of the Oath. Judah went ahead to meet Joseph and prepare the land of Goshen, which Joseph had chosen as their new home. Goshen was a good place for them because it was fertile and close to Joseph, making it ideal for their livestock and families.

These were the family members who traveled with Jacob to Egypt:

- Reuben, Jacob's firstborn, and his sons: Enoch, Pallu, Hezron, and Carmi—four in total.
- Simeon and his sons: Jemuel, Jamin, Ohad, Jachin, Zohar, and Shaul (whose mother was a Zephathite woman)—seven.
- Levi and his sons: Gershon, Kohath, and Merari—three.
- Judah and his sons: Shela, Perez, and Zerah—three.
- Issachar and his sons: Tola, Phua, Jasub, and Shimron—four.
- Zebulun and his sons: Sered, Elon, and Jahleel—three.

These were the descendants of Leah, along with their sister Dinah, who were born to Jacob in Mesopotamia. Including Jacob himself, thirty members of Leah's family entered Egypt.

From Zilpah, Leah's maidservant:

- Gad and his sons: Ziphion, Haggi, Shuni, Ezbon, Eri, Areli, and Arodi—seven.
- Asher and his sons: Imnah, Ishvah, Ishvi, Beriah, and their sister Serah—six.

Zilpah's descendants who traveled to Egypt numbered fourteen.

From Rachel, Jacob's beloved wife:

- Joseph, who had two sons in Egypt, Manasseh and Ephraim (born to Asenath, daughter of Potiphar, priest of Heliopolis)—two.
- Benjamin and his ten sons: Bela, Becher, Ashbel, Gera, Naaman, Ehi, Rosh, Muppim, Huppim, and Ard—ten.

Rachel's descendants who entered Egypt totaled fourteen.

From Bilhah, Rachel's maidservant:

- Dan and his sons: Hushim, Samon, Asudi, Ijaka, and Salomon—five (though only Hushim survived after arriving in Egypt).
- Naphtali and his sons: Jahziel, Guni, Jezer, Shallum, and Iv—five (Iv was born after the famine years but passed away in Egypt).

Bilhah's descendants totaled twenty-six.

In total, seventy of Jacob's family members traveled to Egypt, including his children and grandchildren. However, five of them—Judah's two sons, Er and Onan, and three others who died without children in Egypt—were buried and counted among the seventy nations of the world.

# Chapter XLV.

Israel arrived in Egypt and settled in Goshen on the first day of the fourth month in the second year of the third week of the forty-fifth jubilee. Joseph traveled to Goshen to greet his father, and when they met, he hugged Jacob tightly and wept on his shoulder. Israel said,

"Now I can die in peace, because I have seen your face and know that you are alive. Praise the Lord, the God of Israel, the God of Abraham and Isaac, who has shown me mercy and kept His promises. It is enough for me that I have seen you. The vision I had at Bethel has come true. Blessed be the Lord, my God, forever and ever."

Joseph and his brothers sat down and ate together in Jacob's presence. Seeing them reunited, sharing a meal, filled Jacob with great happiness. He thanked God, who had watched over him and kept all twelve of his sons safe.

Joseph arranged for his father, brothers, and their families to live in Goshen, specifically in Rameses and the nearby areas, which were under his control as Pharaoh's ruler. Israel and his family settled in the most fertile part of Egypt. Jacob was 130 years old when he arrived, and Joseph made sure they had enough food throughout the remaining years of famine.

As the famine continued, Joseph collected all the land in Egypt for Pharaoh in exchange for food. He also took the people's livestock and possessions for Pharaoh. When the famine finally ended, Joseph provided the Egyptians with seed in the eighth year so they could plant again. The Nile had finally overflowed its banks, marking the end of the food shortage. During the seven years of famine, the river had failed to flood, only watering the edges of the land. But now, it once again covered the fields, allowing the Egyptians to grow crops and harvest an abundance that year. This was the first year of the fourth week of the forty-fifth jubilee.

Joseph established a law in Egypt that required one-fifth of all harvests to go to Pharaoh, while the remaining four-fifths were for the people to use as food and seed. This law remained in place for generations.

Israel lived in Egypt for seventeen more years, reaching a total age of 147 years, or three jubilees. He passed away in the fourth year of the fifth week of the forty-fifth jubilee. Before he died, he gathered his sons, blessed them, and told them what would happen in Egypt and in the future. He gave each of them a blessing and granted Joseph a double portion of inheritance in the land.

Israel was buried in the double cave in Canaan, near his father Abraham, in the tomb that Abraham had prepared in Hebron. Before his death, Israel gave all his writings and the books of his ancestors to Levi, instructing him to protect them and pass them down through future generations so they would never be lost.

# Chapter XLVI.

After Jacob passed away, his descendants thrived in Egypt. Their families grew quickly, and they became a large, united people. The brothers cared for one another, and everyone worked together to support their community. During Joseph's lifetime, they increased greatly in number over ten cycles of seven years. There was no trouble or conflict because the Egyptians respected and valued the Israelites while Joseph was alive.

Joseph lived to be 110 years old. He spent 17 years in Canaan, 10 years as a servant, 3 years in prison, and 80 years as a ruler in Egypt. Before he died, he made the Israelites promise that when they eventually left Egypt, they would take his bones with them. He knew the Egyptians would not allow him to be buried in Canaan.

This was because King Makamaron of Canaan, who was living in Assyria at the time, had fought against the Egyptian king in a valley and defeated him, forcing him to retreat to the gates of 'Ermon. However, Makamaron was unable to enter Egypt because a new, stronger ruler had taken power. The gates of Egypt were heavily guarded, and no one was allowed to pass through.

Joseph died in the forty-sixth jubilee, during the sixth week, in the second year, and he was buried in Egypt. Eventually, all of his brothers passed away as well, along with their entire generation.

In the forty-seventh jubilee, during the second week of the second year, the king of Egypt went to war against the king of Canaan. Around this time, the Israelites took the remains of Jacob's sons, except for Joseph's, and buried them in the double cave on the mountain. Most of the Israelites returned to Egypt, but a few stayed in the mountains of Hebron, including Amram, your father, who remained with them.

Later, the king of Canaan defeated the Egyptian king and sealed off Egypt's borders. Afterward, he created a harsh plan against the Israelites. He told his people, "The Israelites have grown too large and strong. We must act now before they increase even more. If war breaks out, they might join our enemies and leave Egypt. Their hearts are already set on returning to Canaan."

To control them, he put slave masters over them and forced them to build strong cities for Pharaoh, including Pithom and Raamses. They were also made to repair and strengthen Egypt's cities. The Israelites were treated cruelly, but the more they were oppressed, the more their numbers grew. This made the Egyptians fear and resent them even more, leading to even harsher treatment.

# Chapter XLVII.

During the seventh week, in the seventh year of the forty-seventh jubilee, your father left Canaan. You were born in the fourth week, during the sixth year of the forty-eighth jubilee. At that time, the Israelites were suffering greatly. Pharaoh, the ruler of Egypt, had ordered that all newborn Hebrew boys be thrown into the river. For seven months, this cruel law was strictly followed, and many baby boys were cast into the waters.

On the day you were born, your mother hid you for three months to keep you safe. When she could no longer hide you, she made a small basket, sealing it with pitch and tar so it would float. She placed you inside and set it among the reeds along the riverbank. For seven days, she returned at night to nurse you, while your sister Miriam stayed nearby during the day to watch over you and protect you from harm.

One day, Pharaoh's daughter, Tharmuth, came to the river to bathe. She heard your cries and told her maids to bring her the basket. When she saw you inside, she felt compassion and decided to adopt you. Your sister stepped forward and asked, "Shall I find a Hebrew woman to nurse the baby for you?" Tharmuth agreed, and Miriam brought your mother, Jochebed, to care for you. Pharaoh's daughter even paid her to look after you.

When you grew older, your mother brought you back to Tharmuth, who raised you as her own son. Although you were brought up in Pharaoh's palace, your father, Amram, secretly taught you how to read and write, making sure you knew your true heritage. You spent 21 years in the royal court, but one event changed your life forever.

One day, while walking outside the palace, you saw an Egyptian beating one of your fellow Israelites. Overcome with anger, you killed the Egyptian and buried his body in the sand to cover it up. The next day, you saw two Israelites arguing and tried to stop them. You asked the one in the wrong, "Why are you hitting your brother?" But he pushed back and said, "Who made you our ruler or judge? Are you planning to kill me like you killed the Egyptian?"

When you heard this, fear took hold of you. You realized that people knew what you had done, and it would only be a matter of time before Pharaoh found out. Worried for your safety, you fled Egypt to escape the consequences of your actions.

# Chapter XLVIII.

In the sixth year of the third week of the forty-ninth jubilee, you left and lived in Midian for five weeks and one year. Then, in the second week of the second year of the fiftieth jubilee, you returned to Egypt. You clearly remember what God told you on Mount Sinai and how Prince Mastêmâ tried to stop you on your way back. He saw that you had been sent to bring judgment on Egypt and used all his power to try and kill you, hoping to prevent you from saving the Israelites. But I rescued you from his grasp, and you carried out the signs and wonders that God had commanded you to perform in Egypt against Pharaoh, his household, his officials, and his people.

The Lord sent powerful judgments against the Egyptians for the sake of Israel. He struck them with plagues: turning the water to blood, covering the land with frogs, tormenting them with lice and gnats, afflicting them with painful boils, killing their livestock, sending hail that destroyed their crops, unleashing locusts that ate whatever was left, covering the land in darkness, and finally, taking the lives of all their firstborn children and animals. The Lord also destroyed their idols, burning them with fire.

Everything happened exactly as you foretold. In front of Pharaoh, his officials, and all of Egypt, you warned them, and each plague came just as you had said. The Lord sent ten devastating plagues to punish Egypt and avenge Israel. He did this to keep His promise to Abraham, repaying the Egyptians for enslaving His people.

But Prince Mastêmâ fought against you the entire time. He tried to hand you over to Pharaoh and helped the Egyptian magicians perform evil tricks. However, we prevented their magic from healing anyone. Instead, the Lord struck them with painful sores so severe that they couldn't even stand, preventing them from performing any more illusions.

Even after witnessing all these miracles, Mastêmâ did not give up. Instead, he encouraged the Egyptians to chase after the Israelites with their full army—chariots, horses, and soldiers. But I stood between them and Israel, protecting My people and delivering them from his hands.

The Lord led Israel safely through the sea, turning the water into dry land so they could cross. But when the Egyptians followed, the Lord threw them into the deep waters, drowning them. Just as they had drowned Israelite children in the river, God repaid them, destroying one million of them, wiping out a thousand strong men for every Hebrew child they had thrown into the water.

On the fourteenth, fifteenth, sixteenth, seventeenth, and eighteenth days, Mastêmâ was bound and held back so he could not accuse the Israelites. On the nineteenth day, we released him, allowing him to influence the Egyptians as they pursued Israel. But God hardened their hearts, making them even more stubborn. This was part of His plan—to bring them to their destruction in the sea.

On the fourteenth day, we bound Mastêmâ so he could not accuse Israel when they took gold, silver, bronze, and clothing from the Egyptians. This was their rightful payment for all the years they had been forced to work as slaves. The Lord made sure the Israelites did not leave Egypt empty-handed.

# Chapter XLIX.

Remember the command the Lord gave you about Passover: celebrate it at the right time, on the fourteenth day of the first month. The sacrifice must be made before evening and eaten that same night, as the fifteenth day begins at sunset.

On this special night—when the festival begins and joy fills the hearts of Israel—you were eating the Passover meal in Egypt. That same night, all the forces of Mastêmâ were released to strike down every firstborn in Egypt, from Pharaoh's son to the firstborn of the lowest servant, even the firstborn animals.

The Lord gave His people a sign: any house with the blood of a one-year-old lamb on its doorframe would be protected. The destroyer would not enter but would pass over, sparing everyone inside because of the blood on the door.

The Lord's power worked exactly as He commanded. The plague passed over the houses of the Israelites, leaving them unharmed. No person, animal, or even a dog suffered any harm. But in Egypt, the disaster was severe—every household lost someone, filling the land with mourning and cries of sorrow.

Meanwhile, the Israelites were eating the Passover lamb, drinking wine, and giving thanks to the Lord, praising Him for their deliverance. They were ready to leave Egypt and escape from their suffering.

Remember this day always, and celebrate it every year on the appointed day, following all the instructions. Do not delay or change the date.

This is an everlasting command, recorded in the heavenly books. Every generation of Israel must observe it every year, on the exact date. This law will never change.

Anyone who is able but refuses to celebrate the Passover on the correct day—failing to offer a sacrifice to the Lord and join in the feast—will be cut off from Israel. Because they ignored the Lord's command, they will bear the guilt of disobedience.

The people of Israel must celebrate Passover on the fourteenth day of the first month, from evening to evening, as the day transitions from light to night. The Lord has commanded that it be observed at this specific time, "between the evenings."

The Passover sacrifice must not be made during the day but only at sunset. It must be eaten that night until the first third of the night has passed. Any leftover meat must be burned.

The lamb must not be boiled or eaten raw. It must be roasted over fire with its head, insides, and legs intact. Its bones must not be broken, for just as no Israelite's bones shall be broken, neither shall the bones of the Passover lamb.

The Lord commanded Israel to observe this festival on its exact date, without postponing it. It is a holy day, a time set apart for worship, and must not be rescheduled or moved.

Tell the people of Israel to celebrate Passover every year, as the Lord commanded. It will be a lasting memorial that pleases Him, and no plague will harm those who keep this command.

The Passover meal must not be eaten outside the Lord's sanctuary. All of Israel must come together and celebrate it at the right time.

Every man who is at least twenty years old on the day of Passover must eat it in the Lord's sanctuary, as it is written. They must partake in the feast before the Lord.

When the Israelites enter the land of Canaan—the land given to them as their inheritance—and establish the Lord's tabernacle in the center of the land, in one of their tribes, they must continue celebrating Passover at the tabernacle every year. They must sacrifice the lamb before the Lord as part of their worship.

When the Lord's temple is built in the land, the people must go there to offer the Passover sacrifice at sunset. The lamb's blood must be placed at the altar's entrance, its fat burned on the altar fire, and its meat roasted and eaten in the courtyard of the holy temple.

Passover must not be celebrated in private homes or in different cities. It must only be observed at the tabernacle or the temple where the Lord's name dwells. The people must remain faithful and not turn away from Him.

Moses, instruct the Israelites to follow these Passover commands exactly as I have given them to you. Teach them to celebrate this festival each year and observe the Feast of Unleavened Bread for seven days. During these seven days, they must eat unleavened bread and bring daily offerings before the Lord at His altar.

This festival is a reminder of the night you left Egypt in haste and entered the wilderness of Shur. You completed the celebration by the sea.

# Chapter L.

After giving you this law, I also told you about the Sabbath days while you were in the desert of Sin, between Elim and Sinai. I explained the Sabbaths for the land on Mount Sinai, and I also told you about the cycle of jubilee years. However, I did not tell you about the year of the jubilee yet because you will only observe it after entering the land that you will possess. The land itself will also observe the Sabbaths while you live in it, and then you will understand the jubilee year.

For this reason, I have established for you the system of weeks, years, and jubilees. There have been forty-nine jubilees from the time of Adam until today, plus one week and two years. There are still forty more years left for you to learn the commandments of the Lord before you cross over the Jordan River into the land of Canaan. The cycle of jubilees will continue until Israel is completely purified from sin, wrongdoing, and impurity. When that time comes, Israel will live in peace, free from Satan and all evil, and the land will remain pure forever.

I have written down the commandment about the Sabbaths for you, along with all the rules and judgments that come with it. You are to work for six days, but the seventh day is the Sabbath of the Lord your God. On this day, no one should work—not you, your children, your servants, your animals, or any visitor staying with you. Anyone who works on the Sabbath must be put to death.

Anyone who dishonors the Sabbath in any way—by engaging in intimate relations, planning work, starting a journey, buying or selling, drawing water that was not prepared on the sixth day, or carrying a load from their house—must also be put to death. You are to do no work on the Sabbath except what was prepared in advance for eating, drinking, and resting. The Sabbath is a day to bless the Lord, who has given you a special and holy day of rest. It is a day for all of Israel to stop working and observe forever.

The Lord has honored Israel by allowing them to eat, drink, and rest on this festival day, free from the labor of men. The only work that should be done on the Sabbath is offering incense, sacrifices, and offerings to the Lord. These acts of worship must take place in the Lord's sanctuary so that atonement can be made for Israel as a lasting memorial that pleases God. These offerings should be presented to Him daily, as He has commanded.

Anyone who works on the Sabbath, travels, tends to their farm, lights a fire, rides an animal, sails a boat, harms or kills any creature, slaughters an animal or bird, catches any fish, fasts, or goes to war on this day must be put to death. This is so the people of Israel will keep the Sabbath properly, as written in the commandments given to me. These laws were recorded on the tablets, teaching the people about the seasons and how to observe their days.

This completes the instructions about how the days are divided.

# Sefer Yetzirah
# (The Book of Creation)

## Introduction to The Book of Creation

The Book of Creation, also known as Sefer Yetzirah, is one of the oldest mystical texts in Jewish tradition. It describes how the universe began, explaining that creation happened through divine wisdom, the Hebrew alphabet, and ten powerful forces called the sefirot. These forces represent different aspects of divine energy shaping the world.

Even though the book is short and filled with mystery, it offers deep ideas about the connection between language, creation, and the divine. Its influence can be seen in later mystical teachings and philosophical ideas about the nature of existence. Including this text in the Apocrypha collection allows readers to explore one of the most fascinating and important discussions about creation in sacred literature.

## Chapter 1

The mirror is not being charitable.

Even with all the noise downstairs—footsteps echoing and voices calling—I lock the door and face the mirror. The glass is covered in smudges and fingerprints, but I can still see myself clearly. I examine my face carefully, like a doctor studying a patient. It's familiar but frustrating.

The dim light doesn't do me any favors, but turning on the overhead lamp would be worse. Its bluish glow would make me look pale and sickly, like I had been pulled out of deep water. That's not the look I need. I have to seem calm, alert, and put together.

My eyes land on my hair—thin, straight, and already greasy, even though I washed it just an hour ago. My fingers reach for the small gray comb in my pocket. A few quick strokes would smooth it down, but I decide to wait until the last moment before leaving. I glance at my forehead—wide and high. Nili calls it "clever," but I never know if she's joking. The smirk on her face when she says it keeps me guessing. If I were as smart as I pretend to be, I wouldn't be in this mess.

Despite washing my face with strong, medicated soap, my forehead is already shiny again. The soap is pink and raw-looking, like uncooked meat, but it does nothing to stop my skin from gleaming. I wonder where all this oil comes from. Which part of me is betraying me? My thick, straight eyebrows arch slightly, as if they, too, are trying to figure it out. I skip over my eyes, unwilling to meet the expression I know is waiting there.

"Telma? Telma!" The doorknob rattles hard. It's Aunt Edith. She hates locked doors. She always needs to know what's going on in everyone's lives, and it makes me uneasy. The family still talks about the time her younger son put a lock on his bedroom door to keep her out. She hired a carpenter to take the whole door off. In response, he called her crazy and moved out. She told everyone that any son who locks her out has no place in her house. They've made up since then, and now she considers herself a parenting expert. I can't stand her.

"Leave me alone," I say, my voice flat but tired. She doesn't argue. Her hurried footsteps tell me she was never planning to push further. Aunt Edith knows when to stop—she's not stupid.

I wonder if it's a mistake to let her wander around the house, poking into things and gossiping. But some fights aren't worth having.

Sometimes, it's easier to give in.

I shift my focus to my nose—small and delicate, but slightly crooked from an old injury. Beneath the skin, tiny pieces of bone shift when I touch them, making a faint rustling sound. In winter, when I blow my nose too hard, pale veins appear along the sides, and a dull pain spreads through it. The ache reminds me that the damage is permanent.

"Telma!" Nili calls from downstairs this time. I ignore her and keep staring at my slightly bent nose. The memory of how it happened still stings, and my cheeks flush. The sudden color makes me look oddly eager.

"You might want to hide this," Nili says from behind the door.

"Hide what?"

"You know." Her voice is teasing, making me rush to the door. "I'll just leave it here." She walks away—not because she respects my space, but because she doesn't want an argument. I open the door and pick up the small book she left. I catch my reflection in the mirror. I don't look happy.

It took a week for anyone to realize my nose was broken. The impact had been unbearable. I saw stars—real ones, not just a figure of speech—green and purple bursts exploding in my vision. I lay still, too humiliated to move, until the stars faded, and I dragged myself to the bathroom. When the water ran pink, I knew it was bad. But since my nose looked normal, I felt relieved.

"So typical," Simon had said later. "As long as it doesn't show on the outside, you don't care. You'd let yourself rot inside as long as you still look fine." He wasn't wrong. Even now, with everything inside me falling apart, I'm obsessed with keeping up appearances. And I think

I'm managing.

The pain in my nose lasted all week, but I assumed it was just bruising. Then, Nili, always blunt, pointed out, "Your nose looks a little off to the left." That's when I was finally taken to the hospital. They put a cold, stiff white cast on it. For two weeks, I carried that weight on my face, clinging to the hope that when it came off, everything would be back to normal.

When the cast finally came off, I looked in the mirror and saw a nose that wasn't mine. Right in the middle sat a small, stubborn bump that hadn't been there before. The shock hit me like another punch. I screamed and argued, refusing to believe it, until they had to calm me down with an injection. They kept telling me it was just swelling, that my nose would go back to normal soon.

Of course, that never happened. Everyone insists my nose looks just as good as before, but I know the truth. That tiny bump wasn't invited, yet there it is, sitting in the center of my face for all to see. Simon, in his usual clueless way, once told me the bump wasn't on my nose—it was in my head. He couldn't be more wrong.

I look at my nose now and try to smile. But somehow, smiling makes the bump stand out even more, so I let my lips relax into their usual tight, pinched shape. They remind me of two little pink snails resting on my chin—one slightly plumper than the other, the top one always dry. Behind them sits my tongue, hidden but sharp, skilled in spinning lies. And today, I already know, will be a day full of them.

I stick my tongue out at the mirror in defiance. "You're such a liar," I say to my reflection. "A master at it. What would I do without you?" My voice drips with sarcasm, but beneath it, there's something close to admiration. Before I can sink any further into this strange moment, a knock at the door startles me. A sharp reminder that life outside this room is still moving, waiting impatiently.

"Telma, we don't have all day!" comes the frustrated voice from the other side. "Hurry up!"

But today isn't just another day, is it? It's different. How often does someone get a test like this—one with no hope, no expectations, no fear of disappointment? I stand in front of the mirror, more exposed than ever before, studying myself like a stranger looking through a microscope. My eyes follow every line and curve of my face.

There they are—my cheeks. Go on, Telma, really look at them. There's no one here to impress. Stop sucking them in.

And there it is, my little double chin, tucked away behind the "real one." Oh, Telma, what's going to happen to you with this round, moonlike face? I sigh, noticing the puffiness in my features. Is it from all the crying last night? Or the endless snacking afterward? All I know is that lifting my head off the pillow this morning felt impossible. As if everything I ate and felt yesterday had settled inside me, thick and heavy, clouding my mind.

I look beneath my eyes—those eyes I still can't meet properly in the mirror. Dark shadows rest there, like bruises that refuse to fade. My skin has taken on a dull, slightly greenish tint, like cheese left in the sun too long. For the first time ever, I feel too pale. Normally, I take pride in my light skin. In this sunny country, I go to great lengths to keep it that way. Few people understand the effort it takes.

Every time I step outside, it's a whole process: oversized sunglasses, a giant hat, and a loose men's shirt to block out the sun. My family—the same people now arguing downstairs as they rush to leave—thinks I'm being ridiculous. They don't know how creative I've become in avoiding the sun. Like that time I forgot my hat at Nili's house and walked home with my head tilted forward, hair covering my face as a shield. I nearly got run over. The car skidded to a stop inches from my feet. The driver, wide-eyed and furious, jumped out to yell at me, but I barely heard him. My mind was somewhere else, picturing something much worse—my body sprawled on the pavement, arms and legs bent in awkward directions, my skin slowly darkening under the sun's harsh rays, like a chicken roasting in an oven.

Oh yes, my face is pale. Very, very pale.

I lower my eyes to my chest, noticing, as always, its slight unevenness. My left breast is just a little fuller, as if my heart is pressing against it from the inside, expanding with each slow beat. Ba-boom, ba-boom, ba-boom. Strange. I thought my heart would be racing today, but it's not. It's steady, unremarkable. I feel a faint tingling in my fingertips and glance at my hands. My hands. I've never liked them. They're small and stubby, with short nails because I can't stop picking at the skin around them. The tiny cuts sting when I touch them.

These hands—always moving, always restless. It's a shame they aren't beautiful, considering they're the part of me I see the most. Nili's hands, though—hers are beautiful. Truly beautiful.

The loud banging on the door snaps me out of my thoughts. This time, Aunt Edith isn't giving up. She pounds her fists against the wood, shouting, "We're all waiting for you! Only you! As always!"

Only you. The words sting, bringing back memories of past scoldings. Like the time I lost my lunchbox with my brand-new sunglasses inside, making everyone tear the house apart looking for it. Only you. Or when I stuck a lollipop in Simon's hair, delaying our trip to the countryside. Only you. And the day I threw up all over the cushions Aunt Edith had spent hours embroidering, making her complain that her eyes nearly fell out from all that stitching.

Yes, Telma. Always you.

But today isn't like those other days. Today, we are getting ready to bury Grandma Gerta. It's her funeral.

I finally lift my eyes to the mirror. My reflection stares back, my gaze a little too bright, holding something I can't quite hide. It almost looks like excitement, though I won't admit it—not even to myself.

# Chapter 8

Grandma, what is this?
A book.
What kind of book?
A very special one.

The Book of Creation now sits on a dusty shelf in the attic, even dirtier than when I first laid eyes on it as a child. Every time it's opened, it seems to absorb something, growing grimier with use. But instead of wearing down, it only becomes stronger—like a body building muscle through exercise. Maybe, dearie, you could have used a little more exercise yourself. This book doesn't lose power when it's used. Instead, it draws from an endless source, growing more potent each time.

This small, ordinary-looking book has bound itself to me in ways I can't explain. It is built on the idea that letters—when connected—can create entire worlds and bring life into existence. Every word spoken, whether out of ignorance, cruelty, curiosity, or indifference, has weight. It brings something new into the world. Even a name, spoken aloud— Telma—has the power to stir something unseen but real.

To you, the idea of letters shaping reality seems obvious, almost natural. What surprises you isn't their power, but the fact that your fragile, breakable body can wield it. Words last longer than you ever will. They are sturdy, unshaken by time—unlike your weak ovaries that may never bear life. Aleph, yod, shin—man. Aleph, shin, heh—woman.

Creation isn't about flesh and blood, about veins and vessels pumping inside you. It is something deeper, more fundamental.

I remember the first time I held the book. A jolt ran through me, like my hands had turned into beams of light. It felt alive, as if I was clutching a tiny, trembling animal—something delicate but powerful, like a kitten with bones as light as air beneath soft fur. It was pure hunger. A raw, desperate need.

I wouldn't let go. Grandma Gerta had to pry the book from my hands. My fingers clenched so tightly that when she finally pulled it away, I was filled with rage. I slapped her. A red mark, shaped like my small fingers, bloomed on her cheek. But she didn't get mad. She didn't even flinch. She just rubbed her face, slowly, knowingly, like she had been expecting this. Like she understood.

I begged her to let me read it. I asked again and again. Each time, she just smiled. But it wasn't her usual smile—it was something different. Something strange, almost affectionate. Her gray-green eyes sparkled like jewels hidden deep beneath the sea. Eyes just like mine.

"Now can I read it?" I would ask.

"Not yet."

"But I'm in third grade now."

"Not yet, kindeleh."

"Then when?"

"You'll know."

Now my eyes are dry, wide open. My mind is sharp, clear, logical. I don't trust anyone—not even myself. I have no patience for people who drift through life like ghosts, their hands always trembling, their voices soft and uncertain. I prefer those who keep their feet firmly planted, even if the ground beneath them is poisoned. People who see the world for what it really is—ugly, cruel, unkind—and do not turn away.

I don't believe in stories or promises. I don't trust words, looks, or even scents. They can all deceive. And I have been deceived too many times, especially by those I once loved.

I am a skeptic. A pessimist. A person who dislikes herself as much as she dislikes others. My disappointment in humanity runs so deep that it has forced my mind open to something else. Something more. There are forces at work beyond what humans can understand, and I feel them moving in the world around me. When I walk through crowded streets, the air hums with something invisible, something living. The rhythm shifts—sometimes slow, sometimes fast. The sun sinks, the sky burns with streaks of gold and fire, and for a moment, everything feels thin, exposed, alive.

I know there are languages beyond words. And you do, too, liar. You talk so fast, tripping over your own tongue, always racing to finish before someone else can cut in. You move quicker than your heart, quicker than your thoughts.

Here I am, locked in my room, tears streaming down my face—thick, cloudy, impossible to hold back. Everyone says Telma is growing up. But TelmaChild has no breasts, no blood, no soft fuzz on her body. She is not a woman. Only an empty, aching space that cannot be filled.

She is small. Round. Trapped in a body that refuses to change, living in a world just slightly off from this one—a world with its own rules, its own unbreakable laws. Under her pillow, she hides a small book, its pages worn thin from use. She sleeps with it close, curled around it as if it is a part of her.

And in her dreams, a single image repeats, again and again. She wakes knowing it is not a dream. But it is not reality, either.

What it is, she cannot say.

In my dream, he stands with his back to me, a dark figure against a world swallowed by flames. Thick smoke fills the air, burning my throat, making it hard to breathe. My lungs tighten, my breath comes in short gasps, and the unbearable heat of destruction surrounds us. But his hands reach for me, gripping tightly, lifting me above the burning ground. The scent of charred wood and the distant sound of collapsing buildings grow louder. His lips meet mine—warm, parted, burning. The air is pulled from my body. My throat tightens. My mouth is dry. Our lips press together, hot and consuming. A kiss. The kiss.

Ash drifts in the smoky air, tiny embers floating around us. My tongue stings—it feels raw, like a scorched, useless thing. He turns, and I slip from his grasp. A building crashes to the ground behind him. His eyes squeeze shut, empty and unreadable.

I wake up suddenly, heart pounding. The house is silent except for the faint creak of footsteps. From the kitchen, I hear my father muttering to himself as he paces across the tiled floor. Shadows stretch along the hallway walls. If this were Grandma's house, I would have wet the bed in fear. Again.

The morning after the pipes burst, the house was eerily quiet. The panic had faded, replaced by something heavier, something unspoken.

"I don't know what caused it," said the plumber Uncle Avrum called in. He held a giant, rust-covered wrench and wiped his boots on the doormat, leaving dark smudges behind.

"I missed all the excitement last night," Nili said, smiling in a way that made my stomach drop. Her tone was too casual. My voice came out dry and rough when I finally spoke.

"What do you mean?" I asked, hoping she was only talking about the pipes.

"Simon seemed pretty shaken up about what happened," she said lightly, as if it didn't matter. I clenched my jaw and said nothing. I refused to let her see how much those words unsettled me, refused to let her glimpse even a fraction of my shame.

"Enough!" Aunt Tzilla's sharp voice cut through the air, startling both of us. Her face was pale, her expression cold and unreadable. She turned her gaze on me. "Have you called Schreiber yet?"

"No. Not yet." I hadn't found the strength to deal with whatever the lawyer had to say.

As I walked through the house, I felt tiny bits of dirt falling from my skin. I hadn't showered since the pipes broke. The dust clung to me like armor, a barrier between me and the world. I wanted to stay this way, wrapped in the filth, until it hardened and cracked on its own, revealing the softer, vulnerable skin beneath. But, of course, that wasn't possible. The eyes around me saw straight through it. They always did.

Schreiber's office was cold, sleek, too polished. Chrome and glass everywhere. Mother and I sank into the deep leather chairs, feeling out of place, feeling dirty. Every tiny movement we made seemed to emphasize how little we belonged here. The secretary approached, as put-together as the office itself. She wore a pale blue angora sweater that hugged her body, matching her soft-colored shoes.

"Can I get you something to drink?" she asked, her voice too smooth, too practiced.

"Coffee," I said flatly. "Three sugars, lots of milk." I watched the slight movement of her sweater as she turned.

"And for you?" she asked, looking at my mother.

"Nothing," Mother whispered, barely making a sound, as if the chair itself was swallowing her whole.

"She'll have coffee too," I snapped, annoyed by the secretary's effortless poise, by the perfect way her life seemed to fit together. I imagined her tangled up with Schreiber on his desk, their sweat mixing with the scattered papers. The thought made my stomach turn.

Schreiber sat across from us, dressed in an angora sweater of his own—maybe a matching set. His voice was smooth, distant, the tone of a man who had dealt with far too many cases like ours.

"Mrs. Sander left a rather unusual condition in her will," he said, his eyes flicking to my mother for a brief moment, as if hinting at the disappointments to come. We already knew the truth—there wasn't much money left.

"She split her bank accounts between her two daughters," he continued, pausing for effect.

"But the apartment on Maharal Street," I interrupted, already knowing what he was going to say, "she left it to me."

Schreiber studied me, his eyes narrowing slightly. "There is a condition," he said, motioning to the secretary. She reappeared, balancing two steaming mugs of coffee on a tray.

"I know what the condition is," I said, keeping my voice steady.

"You do?" Mother's eyes widened, her shock barely contained. I could already see the panic building in her, the realization of what this meant. Aunt Tzilla would be furious. The rich never take it well when something they think belongs to them is taken away. On the way home, Mother would wail in the car, dabbing at her face with a crumpled tissue. But for now, she just stared at me like I was something unfamiliar—something rare and unexpected. Lucky. That was the word running through her mind. She looked at me as if I had somehow become special.

What a fool she was.

"I have to move in," I said calmly. "Right after the seven days of mourning are over. And I have to live there alone. Isn't that right?"

Schreiber hesitated only for a second before nodding. "Yes, that's the main requirement." His voice remained smooth, neutral. He picked up his glass of water and took a slow sip, his movements clean, measured, practiced. Everything about him was careful, controlled. It almost made me like him—despite the sweater, despite the secretary, or maybe even because of them.

"And what if I say no?" I asked, though I already knew the answer. Beside me, Mother tensed, her breath hitching.

But I didn't need Schreiber to respond. There was no room for refusal. No loophole in the will. Just like there was no mention of the real inheritance my grandmother had left me—the one hidden away in the attic. Small, tattered, waiting for me.

On the way home, Mother's awe turned into irritation. She glared at me, her excitement fading into quiet resentment. She hated conflict. So did I, if I was being honest. In that way, we were alike. But that similarity meant nothing now.

Because one thing was certain.

I was going to live in Grandma Gerta's house.

I was going to take her place.

# Chapter 12

The white tablecloth is stained with wine, its surface blotchy and smeared like an old bandage. Passover Seder doesn't feel like a celebration—it feels like a battlefield, filled with spilled wine and simmering resentment.

I pour myself another glass, letting the deep red liquid flood my body, dulling the sharp edges of my thoughts. It's the only way to survive this long, suffocating night of endless rituals and restless hours.

Why is this night different from all other nights? The familiar words ring out across the table. How, indeed? What makes this night different? Bitter matzo? Sharp, lingering fear? Unspoken tensions? A metallic taste lingers in my mouth, a mix of wine and something sharper, something almost like blood. Drink, Telma. Drink more. You haven't had enough yet. Your mind is still too clear. You can still see through their masks.

I look around at faces so much like my own, chewing matzo balls, dribbling greasy broth onto their chins. A room full of people pretending this night is sacred, as if they're anything other than a tangled mess of history, obligation, and quiet contempt.

And yet, look who's judging.

The dirt on my skin, the grime beneath my nails—it's my armor. I let it settle into me, let it hide beneath my crisp white holiday blouse. If someone planted a field of potatoes around my collar, they'd probably grow. Later, when I peel this blouse off, the inside will be speckled with tiny brown spots of sweat and dust, proof of everything I try to bury.

I stare at the jagged piece of matzo in my hand. Its uneven surface is dotted with dark spots. Just burn marks from the oven? Or something else? The old whispers creep into my mind, the accusations, the horrifying stories passed down in secret. Could it be true? Could we be capable of such things? I scan the faces at the table, wondering how many of them would hesitate before picking up a knife. Not many. Maybe not even me.

I take a bite. The edges scrape against my tongue, rough and unyielding. My mouth fills with that bitter, metallic taste again. I swallow.

Something is here. Watching. Waiting. It's been here all along, hiding in the cracks of the ceramic casserole dish at the center of the table or clinging to the walls of my chest. I don't know where, but I can feel it.

We sit stiffly, dressed in our best clothes, surrounding a table heavy with food and tension. We sing the songs, just as we're supposed to: Why on this night do we eat only bitter herbs? Generations of self-loathing Jews like me have sung this same song, sitting at tables just like this one, surrounded by people who claim to be family. No night exposes the weight of family obligations like Passover, where every word spoken, every forced smile, adds to the unspoken debts we pretend not to owe each other.

I glance around the table at the familiar faces. What ties me to these people? Mother. Father. Aunt Tzilla. Uncle Avrum. Nili. Simon. Simon's distant parents. His clueless brother and his scheming wife, along with their three sticky-fingered children. Just listing them in my mind exhausts me.

The men recline in their chairs as tradition dictates, leaning into the pristine white pillows that make Aunt Tzilla's living room feel strangely like a brothel rather than a place of worship. Father's pillow is limp, barely filled, while Uncle Avrum's is thick and luxurious. Even tonight, a night supposedly about freedom, the hierarchy remains clear.

At the center of the table, the roasted chicken leg sits blackened and shriveled, resembling the charred limb of a child. My stomach turns. I swallow another gulp of wine to push down the nausea.

The hagaddah in my hands offers no comfort. A red-haired Moses glares at me from the pages, his cartoonish face twisted with fury. Beside him, massive waves rise, swallowing tiny, screaming figures whole. Later tonight, I know their faces will follow me into my dreams. Every holiday drags ghosts of past celebrations behind it, trapping me in an endless cycle. No matter how old I get, I'm still just a shadow of my younger self.

Another glass of wine is poured. Drink it, Telma. Drink until the emptiness inside you overflows. Maybe the fear will fade. I force it down, wincing. Across the table, Nili watches me, her lips curling into a knowing smile. She sits beside Simon in the chair that used to be mine, comfortable in the space I once occupied. She thinks she's won.

I am nothing but a little girl who has, once again, lost the afikoman prize.

"For finding the afikoman this year, little Telma, what would you like as your reward?"

Father leans toward me, his voice filled with both pride and uncertainty. He isn't used to leading these gatherings, to playing the role of the patriarch.

I look at him, but all I can think about is how easily I've been replaced. By Nili. By Simon's family. By everyone.

"I want a red scooter," I say quietly, already bracing for the disappointment that always follows.

"No problem," Father replies, too eager, too proud. "Whatever you want, you'll get."

There's something new in his eyes—a rare moment where he seems to like himself, to enjoy playing the generous father.

He starts the traditional search for the afikoman, lifting pillows, peeking behind plates, but we all know he won't find it. That's the unspoken rule of Passover: parents aren't supposed to find it, no matter how carelessly it's hidden. It's a ritual. A game that lets children hold a small, temporary power over the adults. Without it, their natural urge to steal or hide would show up in far worse ways.

I think of the times I stole coins from Mother's old, faded purse.

And then, the impossible happens.

Father finds it.

He lifts the napkin-wrapped matzo, holding it in his hands like something foreign, something wrong. He doesn't move. He doesn't speak. He just stands there in the middle of the room, and if I had been paying closer attention, I would have noticed how badly his hands were shaking.

The tears don't come right away. I am still gathering air, my small chest rising, preparing for the wail that will follow. My eyes are wide, my braids framing a face frozen in confusion.

Across the table, Aunt Tzilla watches Father with quiet disgust.

Nili, already pleased with the fancy makeup kit she received as her prize, giggles softly.

Mother leans toward Father, her whisper like a blade slicing through the air. "Oh, Reuven," she hisses, disappointment dripping from every syllable.

And then, at last, the sobs break free.

Tears pour down my hot cheeks as I cry, my voice trembling with betrayal.

"Why did you find it, Daddy? Why? Yucky Daddy!"

My dream of a red scooter crumbles, replaced by something far worse: the realization that my own father has let me down.

He doesn't move. He just stands there, holding the afikoman like it has turned to dust in his hands. If I weren't blinded by my own tears, I might have noticed the way his face changed—the regret settling in, the quiet shame. He hadn't meant to find it. He only wanted, for once, to be the hero. To feel like a winner, even if just for a moment.

The red scooter was bought. It sat in the corner of the living room, bright and untouched, like a monument to that night. The first time I rode it, I fell hard, scraping my ankle so badly that blood spilled onto the pavement, pooling like some kind of strange offering. After that, I refused to ride it again. It stayed there for years, covered in dust, a silent reminder of something I didn't want to think about.

Why on this night do we eat only bitter herbs? The words echo in my mind, their melody turning into something cruel. A reminder of just how deep the bitterness really goes.

I drop my gaze to the hagaddah in my lap. The letters blur, and I'm grateful for it. This night will be easier to get through if I don't have to see the words. I've had enough of words—the ones in this book, the ones in the forbidden book I hid away, the ones I never dared to read aloud. They all have too much power over me.

Moses stares at me from the page, his red hair flaming with righteous anger. His cartoonish face twists in accusation. Look at yourself, he seems to say. Drunk at the Seder table. Is this how a proper Jewish girl behaves? As if your other sins weren't enough, now you have to add this to the list?

"Ssssimon," I slur, my tongue slow and heavy in my mouth. "That's a beautiful sssshirt." I drag out the words, letting them hang in the air, watching them land. There's no point pretending anymore. Once everyone realizes how drunk you are, the need to keep up appearances disappears. And with that, at least, comes a little relief.

"I picked it out for him," Nili cuts in smoothly, her voice filled with pride. "We went shopping yesterday, and I told him we weren't leaving without that navy blue shirt. It's perfect for him—it really makes his eyes stand out."

No one flinches at her casual use of we. Aunt Tzilla and Uncle Avrum lean in, interested, eager for more details about this new connection. Simon's parents, Manny and Batya, don't notice anything at all. They're too busy shoveling food into their mouths, fat glistening on their chins, pooling beneath their skin with each greedy bite. Mother sits quietly, picking at her stuffed chicken, digging into it as though it's done something to offend her. She won't look at me. But her hands keep moving, tearing at the lifeless bird, pulling it apart piece by piece. She knows what's happening. She just refuses to acknowledge it.

Father sits beside her, gnawing on a bone, his face turned away. He won't look at me either.

"So, Telma," Uncle Avrum says, his voice dripping with fake interest, his shirt stained with gravy. "What's going on with you these days? You're thirty now, right? Don't you have a nice young man yet?"

No, Uncle Avrum, there is no "nice young man." I don't want someone nice. I want someone messy, someone whose soul is dark and tangled, someone who understands the chaos inside my head. I want—

If I wanted to, I could stretch my foot under the table, let it brush against Simon's leg. He's sitting right across from me, chewing methodically, his jaw working like a machine. For the first time, I really look at him—at the way he eats, at the way his body glistens with sweat, at the almost animalistic way he consumes everything in front of him.

Seder night turns us all into something less than human.

I glance under the table, half-expecting to see my legs ending in hooves.

"I'm doing just fine, Avrum," I finally say, forcing a tight smile. The wine hasn't loosened my tongue enough to say what I really think, to tell him to drown himself in a bathtub. Those words stay locked inside, like so many others.

Aunt Tzilla's voice cuts through the air, sharp and laced with amusement. "Maybe things will be easier for you now," she says, her earrings catching the light. I notice for the first time how heavy they are, how they pull at her earlobes, dragging them downward. "You've got your own apartment now, don't you? Seems like a good deal for some lucky young man."

I feel my face heat up. The entire room flushes red—anger, embarrassment, and something else I can't quite name.

"What's with that look?" she presses. "Come on, you have to admit—it's a great deal for you. And honestly, you need it more than Nili does. Maybe that's why my mother left it to you."

What does she know about Grandma Gerta's wishes? Nothing. Absolutely nothing. But they hang in the air, invisible but heavy, waiting for someone to say them out loud.

I keep my face blank, my eyes fixed straight ahead. My mother looks small, defeated, her shoulders slumped like the weight of this conversation has crushed her. My father is no better—his eyes flicker nervously between Nili and Simon, but he says nothing. Neither of them does. Maybe they want to. Maybe they don't know how. Maybe it's easier to stay quiet. Either way, their silence says more than words ever could. Why couldn't they be different?

Their weakness drains me, pulling at whatever strength I have left. When the blood is weak, the soul is weak too.

I feel exposed, drowning in my own frustration. My body doesn't feel like my own—my breasts too firm, my hair too long, my skin prickling with discomfort. I hate this moment. It's like the part of the hagaddah I always get stuck reading, the passage filled with words that make my stomach twist. Somehow, every year, it lands on me, forcing me to read aloud the most embarrassing lines. It's like peeling back my own skin, layer by layer, leaving me raw and open.

Words like blood, menstruation, pubic hair—they come tumbling out, each one slicing through me, forcing me to put every awkward, shameful part of myself on display.

"Look, Mother, I have hair down there!" I had once said, young and naive, only to be met with her disgusted reply: "Don't act like a pig!"

But I am a pig. A small, foolish pig. And tonight, my afikomen burns in an invisible fire. I feel wrong, incomplete—like a woman who has waited too long for something she can't even name.

At the center of the table, Elijah's cup sits untouched, gleaming silver, almost sacred. I can't look away. What would happen if I drank from it? Would Elijah appear in a flash of light, furious at my disrespect? Or would nothing happen at all, except for the looks of horror on everyone's faces?

I'm tired of these rituals. Tired of this night that repeats itself year after year. Why do we keep coming back to this table, saying the same words, pouring wine into a cup that no one will ever drink from? My skin itches with tension, my whole body coiled tight like a spring. And then, before I even realize what I'm doing, I stand up.

I reach for Elijah's cup.

"Cheers!" I announce, my voice ringing in the silence.

Every head turns. Simon and Nili freeze. Aunt Tzilla's mouth falls open. My father, mid-bite, chokes on a tiny bone.

"To Grandma Gerta!" I say, louder now. "To the great freedom fighter who led the Warsaw Ghetto Uprising fifty years ago today! To Gerta!" The words tumble out faster. "To Gerta!" And before anyone can stop me, I tilt the cup back and drain it in one gulp.

The wine burns as it slides down my throat, but at least it doesn't taste like blood.

The silence is suffocating. They stare at me, horrified, their mouths slightly open, as if I've broken some unspoken law. They look like fish gasping for air, wide-eyed and wordless. In their eyes, I've confirmed every low expectation they've ever had of me.

I keep drinking as the night drags on, trying to drown the strange feeling rising inside me. But what am I waiting for? I don't even know.

I stumble into the kitchen. The countertops, wrapped in tin foil for Passover, glint under the harsh light, making the whole room look cold and sterile, like a morgue. I turn on the faucet, letting the water run over my hands, as if I can wash away the tension. But some things don't come clean.

A voice inside me whispers, Turn around.

And I do.

Through the open door, I see them—Nili and Simon—standing together on the tiny balcony.

They're close. Too close.

Simon's voice is hesitant. "I don't know if we should be doing this."

But Nili touches his arm, tilts her head toward him. Under the streetlight, their figures fit together perfectly, like the couple on a greeting card. And then, just like that, they kiss.

Slow. Deep. Real.

I don't move. The wine doesn't blur it. I see everything. My hands clench into fists, but I can't look away. It's beautiful. The most perfect kiss I've ever seen.

But it's not mine.

And just like that, something inside me snaps.

A wave of nausea hits, and suddenly, everything I've eaten and drunk comes rushing up. Matzo balls, sweet carrots, horseradish, wine—it all surges out, splattering onto the kitchen floor. Onto Nili's dress.

The mess clings to her like an accusation.

I collapse, shaking, too stunned to care.

Aunt Tzilla runs in, screaming about her ruined kitchen. My mother looks at me, silent, disappointed. Then, as always, she turns away.

I stay on the floor, covered in filth, feeling nothing.

But then, slowly, I push myself up.

I am not dead. Not yet.

Anyone who can pretend, who can keep playing the game, isn't truly gone.

I stumble out of the house, past the staring eyes, past Simon, who won't even look at me. I step into the night. The tears don't come. They harden inside me into something else.

I run.

I know exactly where I'm going.

And this time, I'm ready.

# Chapter 13

The soil in the cemetery is dark and heavy. Above, a blood-red moon hangs in the sky.

You move with purpose, your entire body focused on what must be done. Every part of you feels alert, buzzing with anticipation. Your chest tightens, your skin tingles. Faster, Telma. Move faster. Your thighs brush together as you push forward.

You are completely clean. You spent the afternoon scrubbing yourself, making sure no trace of dirt remained. You scrubbed everywhere, but you paid special attention to that secret, delicate place between your legs—the hidden part of you, soft and red, always kept out of sight.

Move, now! You break into a run. Every step feels urgent, every second precious. In the distance, buildings crumble, sending sparks flying dangerously close. Laughter echoes from the darkness, sharp and familiar. The voices taunt you, their sing-song words floating through the night:

From earth and blood you knead the dough
    Watch until it rises so…

You ignore them. There's no time for their nonsense. You dig your fingers into the soil, clawing at the ground, your nails cracking against the hardened dirt. Faster, Telma. They're coming. You can feel them getting closer. The sharp smell of smoke stings your nose, burns your throat. The earth resists, but you push on, dragging water from the basin near the purification room. The water runs pink, stained with something old, something powerful.

With steady hands, you shape him from the damp soil. Every curve, every line—you know them all. You've seen him before, in your mind, in your dreams. There is no room for mistakes. Not this time.

From earth and blood you knead the dough
  Watch until it rises so…

The rhyme lingers, but you block it out. Your hands move on their own, driven by something deeper than thought. Maybe it's the lifeless body before you, calling you forward. Maybe it's the force inside you, pulling both of you toward something unstoppable.

Your fingers mold the shape of his shoulders, the curve of his neck, the broadness of his chest, the strength of his thighs. His body is smooth, powerful, strong—even though he is still only earth. But you know exactly what he must become, and you shape him without hesitation. Every motion feels like destiny, as if you've always known how to do this.

When you finally step back, he lies still on the ground. His quiet presence pulls you in. He looks peaceful, lost in a deep sleep. He has no idea what's coming. Neither do you. Not really. But your breath quickens as a memory flashes through your mind—the heat of a kiss, the way it drowned you, swallowed you whole. The thought almost breaks your focus, but you push it aside.

There is still more to do. And this time, you are sure of yourself.

You no longer wear the wedding dress. You know now that it was never the key to success. You are no one's bride. Not yet.

You begin to move, stepping carefully around him, tracing a perfect circle in the dirt. Once. Twice. Seven times. Your feet stay firm, your body steady. The words flow easily from your lips, etched into you like fire. Each sound carries power, each syllable feels alive. Beneath you, his body begins to glow. At first, it's only faint, like an ember catching light. Then, the glow deepens, as if breath is filling his form.

You don't stop. You keep circling. Seven more times. The air thickens, charged with energy. The world feels like it's waiting, holding its breath.

Then, the final moment arrives.

You lean over him, your lips forming the sacred word—the Name of Names, the word that seals creation.

Your mouth is dry, cracked from the force of your voice, but you don't stop. He is balanced on the edge of existence, and with this final act, everything will change.

You want this. You need this.

His body begins to shift. Water seeps into the earth, steaming and hissing, surrounding him in a mist. It looks like he might disappear into smoke, but you don't let it distract you. Your feet keep moving, circling again and again. The dizziness threatens to take over, but you push through it. Fool! you scream at yourself. Just this once, do something right!

Then, you see it.

Dark hair begins to spread over his body—thick, strong, alive. Fingernails and toenails emerge from the skin, twenty perfect crescents, gleaming in the dim light. They are flawless, whole, real.

And they move.

"Focus," you whisper to yourself, barely making a sound, afraid that even the smallest noise might break the delicate moment. Just a little longer. You're almost there.

Around you, the letters swirl like a raging storm, shifting, pulsing, alive with purpose. A large, rotting peach floats nearby, its sickly-sweet scent filling your nose, making your stomach turn. The two-headed child watches again, its teary, haunting eyes cutting through your concentration. In your hand, the small slip of paper shakes, almost burning through the bag that held it. Was this how it happened for her? Was this how Grandma Gerta did it all those years ago?

The thought flickers for only a second before you push it away. There's no time for doubt.

Carefully, you remove the sacred parchment and slip it into the mouth you shaped with such precision.

The lips tremble as the paper disappears inside. Full, perfect lips— so pure, so untainted. Could something so flawless ever tell a lie? But you don't let yourself wonder. Not now. You steady yourself and begin to recite the words again, each syllable slow and deliberate. You know that one wrong sound could ruin everything.

A faint noise—wet, raw, almost like the first gasp of a newborn— breaks the silence. The final piece has fallen into place. You lean in, your voice barely above a whisper:

"And He breathed into his nostrils the breath of life, and man became a living soul."

And then, you wait.

Waiting has become part of you, as natural as breathing. You know it well. It is woven into the deepest parts of your being.

He lies before you, still and smooth, his lips sealed. Nothing happens. The air grows thick with the weight of failure. You start to accept the inevitable—that you are alone, that you were always meant to be alone.

Your knees give out, and you sink to the ground. There are no tears. Even that would be too much effort. You press your face into the dirt, letting its coolness offer whatever comfort it can. You will stay here until you disappear, until the last bit of hope inside you is swallowed by the earth.

And then—you hear it.

Faint. Subtle.

A heartbeat.

Your lips, still buried in the dirt, rest against his chest. The warmth spreads beneath you. Alive. You lift your head in shock. His chest rises and falls. His heartbeat grows steadier, stronger. He breathes.

Your own heart pounds in response.

Then, he moves.

His limbs tremble, his eyes flutter open—dark and rich, the color of the soil itself. His gaze meets yours, and for a moment, something flickers in them before vanishing. He stretches his arms, shifts his body, his movements slow but full of power. And then, he stands.

Towering over you.

The golem has risen. The man you created with your own hands, shaped by your own will.

You push yourself to your feet, tilting your head back to meet his eyes. The moon is gone now, swallowed by the night.

This is the moment. You must name him.

You take a breath, steadying yourself. The name has been inside you all along, waiting for this very moment. Every letter must be right—every sound must fit the body you brought into being. A mistake would leave him incomplete, broken. And after all this, you refuse to accept anything less than perfection.

Your lips part. They are dry, trembling.

You swallow. And then, you speak.

"Saul."

The name barely leaves your lips, yet it carries weight.

Saul—the borrowed one. The man who is not yours to keep.

His eyes lock onto yours. And you know—he understands.

The streets are eerily quiet. The night feels darker than ever. It is almost as if fate has cleared the way, ensuring that no one is there to see you lead this towering, naked form toward home. You wrap him in an old tarp, found behind the purification room, and together you walk through the empty streets.

The air is thick with the scent of citrus—blooming orange trees mixed with the sweetness of rotting peaches. The wild fragrance of flowers fills the silence. Saul pauses, his eyes wide, drinking in the world as if seeing it for the first time. You catch his expression and feel something strange rise inside you.

You smile.

But just as you reach the entrance of your building, something catches your eye.

A lifeless bird.

Its gray feathers are tangled with red, its small body broken, its beak frozen open in an eternal, silent cry.

You stop.

A chill runs through you.

The night feels heavier now, pressing down with the weight of creation—and the weight of what comes next.

# Chapter 14

The apartment feels strangely alive, like it's holding its breath. My eyes drift around the room, stopping on the old wooden dresser from Warsaw, the towering stack of religious books, the heavy rug covered in dust, the embroidered fawn trapped behind a glass frame. Everything is still, quiet, as if waiting.

I did it. My body is tense, my eyes bright, like a kid suddenly taken seriously as an adult. I stand in the middle of this dingy room, taking in the drooping plants and the sticky floor covered in smudged fingerprints. Crumbs roll across the ground—leftovers from some forgotten snack. This place is a mess. How could anyone visit here? And yet, I'm not alone. Someone else is watching, his eyes scanning the room. Will this be his home one day? His face gives nothing away, blank and unreadable. But then, his gaze shifts—upward, toward the attic. There's something sharp in his expression, something questioning. He sees more than I expected. I look away, embarrassed. My pride, my guilt, my uncertainty—it's all mixed up inside me, swirling between fear and hope.

But still, I did it. Somehow, I actually made this happen.

The air between us feels heavy. He's standing so close now that I take a step back without thinking. He's tall, solid, like a statue come to life. His deep brown eyes roam over my pale skin, searching for something. I don't know what. And whatever it is, he doesn't seem to find it. He just waits. His eyelashes are so perfect, they look like they were sewn on by hand.

But wasn't I the one who made him?

The thought won't leave my head. Me, me, me. I built him with my own hands. He's here, breathing, moving, because of me. I want him to scoop me up, to lift me off the ground.

But he doesn't.

We just stand there, waiting, caught in the same silent moment.

Memories rush back—me and Simon, running to the cemetery the night after Grandma Gerta died.

"You'll see," I had told him, buzzing with confidence. "It's going to work this time. Just wait."

"What if it comes alive and attacks us?" Simon's voice had shaken. "They say golems are unbelievably strong, and they always end up in violent situations. What if it's angry that we brought it to life without asking?"

His fear had been real. And, honestly, it was no surprise we failed that night. Fear always kills creation. Always.

But me? Was I fearless?

"You don't get it," I told him, practically shaking with excitement. "The best part about making a golem is that we control everything. It doesn't move or even blink unless we tell it to. That's what makes it so amazing."

What a fool I was.

Now, the last thing I want to do is give orders. I don't know how. The only commands I've ever given are to my parents—"Open the window!" or "Move, that's my seat!" or "Where's my gray skirt?"

Everyone else? I only order them around in my head. Trip and fall. Disappear. Burn in hell. But, of course, no one ever listens.

And him? I can't do it. I won't. What would I even say?

His stare doesn't waver, challenging me. "Go on," his eyes seem to say. "Give me a command."

"Umm... uh... go to the kitchen," I mumble, barely above a whisper.

Will he listen?

His body shifts, his movements smoother now, no longer stiff like before. He walks through the parlor with ease, stopping by the sink, like he's been here before. And that's when I realize—I didn't need to tell him where to go. He already knew.

A hundred questions flood my mind, but I push them aside. Instead, I follow him, drawn toward the stove, feeling the sudden urge to cook for him.

What a fool I am.

The dining table is set with the fancy china—the ones with red flowers that look like fresh wounds. I'm nowhere near as good at cooking as Nili, so I keep it simple. Slices of oranges and peaches, uneven from my clumsy hands. Matzos, sharp-edged and brittle, like something ready for battle.

He stands motionless by the sink, in the exact spot where I once stood kissing Simon. The memory feels distant, unimportant—like something out of an old book. On this date, in this apartment, such-and-such happened. But who cares? What does it matter now? Simon barely reached the spice rack. Saul, though—his head nearly touches the tallest cupboard.

I'm glad I used so much dirt. If you're going to create something, you should do it properly. I remember the effort—digging, scraping, shaping. My hands still ache from it, my broken nails stinging from the dirt trapped underneath. Saul's dark eyes drop to my hands, noticing. I quickly brush them clean, letting the dirt fall to the floor.

His body flinches, just barely, at the sound. His face stays unreadable.

Why isn't he sitting? The realization sinks in, draining me. I say the word, "Sit," and he does. No hesitation. The huge figure lowers himself into the chair, but his gaze stays locked on my hands, like he's waiting for me to tell him to pick up the fallen dirt.

I don't. Not yet.

I grab a peach and bite into it, the soft flesh giving way beneath my teeth. My stomach twists, unsure if I'm hungry or just anxious. Saul doesn't move. His eyes follow the pink juice running down my chin. He does nothing to help. Nothing at all.

"Eat," I whisper, urging him.

Still, he doesn't move.

Frustrated, I cut a small piece of peach and place it in his hand. He stares at it, his expression shifting—was that sadness? "It's really good," I say, trying to encourage him. "Go ahead, eat." But he doesn't.

I try again, this time using a fork to lift a slice to his lips. But when I press it against his mouth, he doesn't open. His teeth don't budge. Then I remember—there's a slip of paper under his tongue, the thing that holds his essence. A cold fear grips me. What if the paper gets damaged? What if he collapses right here, turning into nothing but a pile of dirt on my kitchen floor? My hand freezes, and the peach slice slips from the fork, rolling down his chest and leaving a sticky trail.

His eyes flicker with something like impatience.

I know offering him coffee is pointless. Instead, I sit across from him, sipping my lukewarm drink in silence. Our so-called meal sits untouched—dried-out peach slices, bits of dirt scattered on the table, old photographs smudged with stains. These ordinary things remind me of my failure. The kitchen feels too quiet, the air too heavy. And then I notice something strange—the birds outside are silent. Their absence gnaws at me, but I shove the thought aside. Not now, Telma. Focus.

I clear the table without asking for help, feeling ridiculous. What kind of person creates a golem only to end up serving him? At this rate, I'll be the one with a slip of paper under my tongue, another mindless servant, another cliché. The thought makes my stomach turn. I bump the table with my foot, spilling coffee all over both of us.

Saul moves instantly. He stands so fast that the table crashes against the wall. Plates shatter, photographs flutter to the floor, and oranges roll across the tiles, bursting and leaking juice. He backs away, pressing himself into a corner, his face frozen in shock as he watches the coffee drip.

I follow his gaze and see it—a small hole forming in his skin where the liquid touched. It's dark and muddy, the edges crumbling.

Panic grips me. I ruined him.

The hole spreads, oozing black sludge. Saul doesn't move, doesn't try to stop it. His wide, trusting eyes beg me for help. I step forward, but as soon as my fingers brush the wound, he jerks back violently, almost knocking me over. He looks at me with unbearable pain, his body trembling. The wound keeps growing, and the sharp smell of damp earth fills the room.

Desperate, I grab a dying houseplant, scooping up its dry soil. Without thinking, I press the dirt into the wound. The moment it touches his skin, it absorbs, sealing the hole.

I let out a shaky breath. It worked.

Saul takes my hand and places it over the spot where the hole had been. His eyes shine with something close to gratitude, and suddenly, I feel ashamed.

What now? The night isn't over, and I still don't know what to do with him. He's a stranger in my home. Where will he sleep? Should I let him into my bed? The thought makes my chest tighten. I don't like sharing my space, and the few times I have, it ended badly.

I hesitate, unsure. What am I supposed to say? What am I supposed to do? I stand there, frozen, overwhelmed by my own choices.

Then, as if he can hear my thoughts, Saul turns and walks toward the attic. I don't stop him. I just watch as his tall, solid figure moves away. I imagine him standing there every night, keeping silent watch while I toss and turn in Grandma Gerta's massive, empty bed. Maybe this is how it's meant to be. Maybe I don't get to decide what's right or wrong anymore.

As he walks, his foot brushes against one of the scattered photographs from the mess earlier. He bends down and picks it up with surprising gentleness. It's an old war photo of Grandma Gerta—the one where her wild, intense eyes stare straight ahead, full of some fierce, private emotion. Saul stares at it, unmoving. Time stretches thin, pulling me back to that night in the cemetery—tripping over uneven ground, everything narrowing into a single, frozen moment. I hadn't needed to read the name on the gravestone. I had already known who was buried beneath it.

Saul lifts the photograph closer, his fingers moving with slow care, as if he's holding something sacred. Then, after a moment, he turns to me.

Without saying a word, he reaches out, his large hands cradling my face. His touch is gentle, careful—like I'm something fragile. He strokes my cheeks, his fingers gliding over my lips with the lightest pressure. His thumb lingers at my lower lip before his whole hand covers my mouth.

For the first time, he looks at peace. Almost… happy.

My eyes flick toward the mirror in the corner. The reflection staring back at me is not my own.

It's her.

Grandma Gerta's fierce face, filled with strength and beauty, gazes back at me. And in that moment, I can't tell where she ends and I begin.

Now I am in bed. My eyes are closed, my lips slightly parted. The air is thick with the scent of hot earth. Ashes swirl in the darkness, brushing against my skin like whispered secrets. Saul leans over me, his breath warm and deep. He pulls me toward him, and then his lips are on mine, firm, unrelenting.

The kiss consumes me.

Our mouths press together, tangled in a feverish need, as though something inside us is burning. My lips tingle, almost as if they're melting under his touch. The heat spreads, searing, as if the kiss itself is made of fire. My skin feels like it's bubbling, soft and fragile.

I know that even when the kiss ends—if it ever ends—we'll still be connected. There will be something between us, thin and stretched tight, impossible to break.

But right now, none of that matters.

Let this kiss last forever, I think. Let it pull me under completely. Let me disappear into it.

Then—

A pounding knock shatters the silence.

My eyes snap open. The world slams back into focus, crushing me beneath its weight.

Someone is at the door, knocking hard. Again and again.

The sound is relentless, sharp, and urgent.

Whoever it is, they need to get in.

Damn it.

"Telma, open the door."

Simon's voice is firm, slicing through the silence. My heart jumps as I leap out of bed and rush to the mirror. My reflection stares back— flushed lips, dark circles under my eyes, and a tense expression I can't shake. It's nothing Simon hasn't seen before, I tell myself. But still, he's the last person I want to face right now. Well, second to last.

I reach the door but hesitate. Not the time for grudges, I remind myself, even though just hearing his voice makes my stomach twist.

"What do you want?" I ask, keeping my voice calm, maybe even a little distant. Just enough to remind him of what he did with Nili— something I haven't forgotten.

"Why didn't you answer my calls yesterday?" His tone is sharp. I can tell he's suspicious.

"I was busy," I say with a shrug.

"With what?" His eyes scan the room, searching for something—

anything—that might explain what's really going on. I lean against the doorframe, trying to look casual, but he pushes past me and steps inside. So much for staying in control.

"Is everything okay?" His eyes narrow as he studies me.

Something in his expression makes me extra careful with my words. "Yeah, I'm fine," I say, steady and even.

But he doesn't believe me. I force a small smile, pretending everything is normal, but it feels forced, unnatural. The effort is exhausting. Even the room feels different, like something's slightly off. Is it just me, or has that mold stain on the wall gotten smaller?

A wave of panic crashes over me. What if Saul suddenly walks out of the attic? The thought is unbearable. Simon seeing Saul—or worse, Saul seeing Simon—is a disaster waiting to happen. But Saul won't come out, right? I haven't told him to. That should be enough. Shouldn't it? I barely know what he's capable of.

Simon needs to leave. Fast.

"What do you want?" I ask again, but this time my voice is tight, high-pitched. Too obvious.

Simon watches me carefully. "Something's up," he says, suspicion dripping from every word. "I don't know what, but... you look different."

Different.

The word lands like a crack in the surface of my mind, shifting the way I see him. For the first time, he seems smaller, paler—his skin dull, like the ghostly white mushrooms that grow in dark places. And his lips... dry, lifeless. Were these the lips that once made my whole body burn? The same lips that used to pull me in so easily?

I stare at them, and they part.

"Telma," he says. "About Seder night—"

Any other day, I might have apologized. I might have played along, told him Nili's dress was an accident, reassured him that he could be with whoever he wanted.

But not today.

"What about Seder night?" I interrupt before he can launch into whatever excuse he's been rehearsing. His face shifts, thrown off. For a second, he just stares at me, confused—like he doesn't understand why I'm not following the usual script.

"I just wanted to make sure you were okay," he says at last, voice uncertain. "I didn't want to leave things like this before I go abroad."

My stomach tightens. "Where are you going?" I ask, keeping my tone light.

"Poland. Today. The March of the Living starts right after Passover this year."

Of course. How could I forget? Another trip to wander through cemeteries, sifting through dirt, chasing the ghosts of our past. Seems like that's the real family tradition.

"Your dad's been after me about some documents from Warsaw," Simon adds. "Something about an old building your family owned. He wants me to track it down while I'm there."

Then—I hear something. A faint sound from the attic.

My head tilts slightly, listening, my body tense. Simon notices immediately. His frown deepens, his suspicion growing.

"Are you sure everything's okay?" His voice is sharper now, pressing me for answers.

I take a breath. And then, before I can stop myself, the words slip out.

"Tell me, Simon," I say, my voice raw. "Do you love her?"

Golem or no golem, I have to ask. Because at the end of the day, Simon was here first. And we're talking about Nili—my cousin, my coworker, my lifelong rival. The girl who always seems to be one step ahead of me.

He hesitates. Then another noise comes from the attic.

"Yes," he finally says. "I think I do."

The words cut straight through me.

Two eyes, two lips, one heart, one emptiness.

Which one is more beautiful? He answers without hesitation.

And suddenly, I find myself capable of giving a command—at least in my mind. Kill! I scream silently. Tear him apart!

But Saul is in the attic. And I am still standing here, face to face with Simon.

He watches me closely, his expression shifting between relief and suspicion. Later, when he's on his flight to Warsaw, he'll probably think, She handled that pretty well. He might even tell Nili.

But what he won't see—what no one will see—is the look on my face once I close the door behind him.

Now is the time for tears.

I've always believed that forcing a smile is the quickest way to make yourself cry. The body reacts, like it has to balance out fake happiness with real sadness. And crying? Crying is easier. Tears are natural. Smiling through pain takes effort.

I sink onto the living room carpet. I could say I soak it with my tears, but the truth is, there are none. My tears don't fall—they cut. They stay locked inside, sharp and jagged, like tiny shards of glass pressing behind my eyes. They scrape and burn, but they never spill over.

I cry for Simon. For Nili. For the years I lost. For Grandma Gerta. For myself. Even for Saul.

How could I have been so blind? I always thought I was weak, but smart enough to make up for it. Smart enough to be dangerous one day. But now I see myself clearly.

I was wrong.

I am small. Unimportant. Forgettable. Unloved.

The pain is unbearable. I collapse onto my hands and knees, my forehead pressed into the carpet. The position is familiar—too familiar. As familiar as the empty space inside me where all my tears should be.

But this time, someone hears me.

He lifts me gently, holding me close.

Saul.

I feel his warmth, steady and strong. His wound has healed—his skin is smooth, unmarked. My hands move over him, searching, but he stops them, holding them in his own. His hands burn like fire.

He tilts my face up toward his.

And then I see it. The sadness in his eyes.

It's for me.

All of it.

A tear finally falls, sliding down my cheek. I want to bury my face in his chest, to lose myself in his warmth, but I hesitate. What happens if my tears touch his burning skin?

Saul moves slowly, brushing them away with his fingers. Mud smears across my skin, and thin wisps of steam rise where his touch lingers. Pain flickers in his eyes, but he is so gentle, so careful, that I can't stop the tears from coming.

Something stirs inside me, small and delicate. It flutters, like a tiny heartbeat. Could this be happiness? I don't know. I have nothing to compare it to.

I look up at him.

My lips tingle, aching for what comes next. The kiss.

The one I've imagined. The one that finally feels real.

I lean in, my whole body drawn to him, and press my lips toward his.

But just before I reach him, Saul turns his head away.

The shock hits me like ice water.

The rejection slams into me, but even worse than the rejection itself is the fact that I never expected it.

This wasn't supposed to happen.

It feels wrong—like a mistake, an error in how things were meant to go. I had been so certain. That certainty was what gave me the courage to reach for him in the first place. And yet, here I am.

Rejected.

In any other situation, I'd be embarrassed. I'd worry about bad breath or food in my teeth.

But not now. Not with him.

Because even as he turns away, he doesn't let go of me. He still holds me close. His body burns against mine, his eyes full of something I can't quite name.

I can feel his desire—it mirrors my own, maybe even greater. But that only makes the rejection more confusing, more painful.

And yet, I know—without a doubt—the kiss already happened.

I felt it. Everywhere.

It filled the air, it filled me.

So why does it feel like it disappeared? Like it was never real?

Where did it go?

And why—why—did he pull away?

The questions won't stop. They press in on me, suffocating. But none of them change the way I feel about him. None of them erase the bond between us, the connection that wraps around me, stronger than anything I've ever known.

And then, just as the thought takes hold, another one crashes through.

A cold, undeniable truth.

He is not a living thing, Telma.

# Chapter 15

Everything that happens to us leaves a mark—inside and out.

What we call "facial features" are really just muscles and tendons waiting beneath the skin, shifting and shaping with every experience. Every feeling, every moment, leaves its trace, telling the world our story whether we want it to or not. Our faces reveal us, exposing things we might prefer to keep hidden. Maybe that's why they wear out so quickly. It's not just aging, like beauty magazines claim—it's the weight of emotions, the constant pull of what we've been through.

It's not gravity that makes a face change. It's life. Eyes that have seen too much grow heavy. A nose that has smelled fear sharpens, as if stretching away from danger. Ears sag, burdened by words they were never meant to hear. Anger clenches a jaw, twisting it into something almost wild. Every line, every shadow, is a road map of everything we've survived.

One day, people might cover their faces the way they cover their bodies. For now, we settle for masks.

And mine? Mine is the ugliest of all.

I stare at myself in the bathroom mirror, studying every curve, every line. My lips, untouched by any kiss, press together tightly, hardened by disappointment. I run my fingers across my skin, feeling the slight slickness of morning oil. Most days, my face is so greasy when I wake up that it feels like a frying pan. But today, it looks calm—giving away nothing. Still, I keep looking, waiting for it to betray me.

As I brush my teeth, Saul appears in the doorway, leaning against the frame. His blurred shape lingers in the mirror, his outline soft behind my sharper reflection. I wipe the steam from the glass, but even then, he stays hazy, like he belongs to another world.

The toothpaste in my mouth turns thick and foamy, and I spit it out, my head tilting back up to find him still watching me.

I should be used to the way he looks at me by now, the way his gaze lingers, slow and deliberate. But this time, it feels different—deeper, more invasive. His eyes don't just glance over me; they seem to reach inside, exploring parts of me I've never shared with anyone.

It's like he's speaking to my insides—my kidneys, my lungs, my ovaries. No matter how many layers I wear, I feel completely exposed in front of him.

And the thought of him seeing me without those layers? It makes my stomach tighten. When will that happen? whispers a voice in my head. You dirty girl.

A naked body can't hide anything. Every scar, every flaw, every secret is out in the open. There's no pretending. No mask.

Saul keeps his gaze on my face, which is now dripping with white foam. I wonder what he's holding inside those closed lips. That tiny slip of paper—small, powerful, unreachable. What happens when I need it back? It's not yours, something inside me reminds me.

I lean closer to the mirror to put in my contact lenses. The thin, glassy discs sting as they settle into place, and the bathroom sharpens around me. My eyes land on a forgotten pair of pantyhose behind the door, already growing mold. On the mirror, a faint circle of steam lingers where my breath touched the glass. Saul stares at it.

Later, I'll catch him in the same spot, breathing against the mirror again and again, as if testing something. His reflection stays clear, unchanged. No fog. No warmth. Not even the faintest sign of breath. He exhales forcefully, trying to make something appear, willing himself to leave a trace of heat in this world.

In the kitchen, I set the table for one, just like I did in my loneliest days. Slices of pink peaches, soft cheese, brown rolls, a perfectly poached egg. I drink cold water straight from the grimy faucet, the icy chill stabbing my teeth. I don't dare spill anything near Saul.

He sits across from me, motionless, silent, eating nothing.

What keeps him going? What fuels this man made of earth? Are the letters under his tongue enough to sustain him, the way certain words steal the breath from my lungs? MY. SAUL. The thought is oddly comforting, though I'd never say it out loud. The idea of becoming one of those lovesick fools, asking if he sees a future with me, if he'll always be mine—it makes me shiver.

Saul watches me. His lips curl slightly, almost like a smirk, as if he can hear my thoughts.

His presence across the table is overwhelming. His form is too solid, too real. The weight of it presses against me, stirring something deep in my stomach—a discomfort so thick it feels like a snail crawling down my thigh, leaving behind a sticky, shameful trail.

I push back from the table, standing abruptly. This has to stop.

I rush to my grandmother's old closet. My grandfather was tall, strong—like Saul. His old suits still hang alongside the summer dresses.

Without thinking, I grab a few shirts and throw them at Saul. Harder than necessary.

I wonder what Grandma Gerta would think if she saw this—if she knew what I was doing with her late husband's clothes.

The thought makes my skin crawl. But I can't stop thinking about it.

I try to picture Grandpa Andrei, but his face is as blurry in my mind as Saul's was in the mirror earlier. All I can remember is a kind smile— one that reminds me of Bella's mischievous grin. But now, I wonder if that smile wasn't pure kindness. Maybe it was the quiet acceptance of someone who lived without love.

Grandma Gerta didn't love him enough. She never looked at him with warmth, never rested her hand on his arm, never laughed with him the way she did in that old wartime photograph. Maybe she only felt alive in moments of danger, in the rush of survival. Maybe a steady, safe love like Andrei's was too dull for her.

And the worst thought of all—am I just like her? Do I need chaos, destruction, and risk to actually feel something?

My hands clench into fists. The dry skin scrapes against itself, rough and peeling. I glance down and notice tiny cracks forming on my knuckles, like my body is reflecting the emptiness inside me.

I lift my eyes back to Saul. He hasn't moved. One of my grandfather's shirts rests on his knees, draped like a napkin at a fancy dinner.

"You need to get dressed," I say. But even as I say it, another thought creeps in. Why? Who else is going to see him but me?

Why cover up something so perfect?

His body is everything I am not. His dark, earthy skin looks like it was shaped straight from the soil of the cemetery, while mine is pale, almost colorless. My round face and weak chin are nothing compared to his sharp, sculpted jawline. The bump on my nose has no match on his perfectly straight profile. His lips are full, rich in color, while mine are thin, like a cruel joke.

And then there's the way he carries himself—tall, steady, unshaken. His strong shoulders hold him upright while I shrink under the weight of my own thoughts. Next to him, the top of my head barely reaches his neck.

It feels right, though.

My eyes drift downward, stopping just before I let myself go too far. Beneath those sculpted muscles, there is more beauty. More strength.

But I can't look.

I tell myself it's because of modesty, because of the way I was raised. But the truth is, I feel a heat pooling deep inside me, a strange shame pressing against my skin.

Being naked must have a reason, I think. It can't just exist without meaning.

"Get dressed," I say again, sharper this time.

Saul picks up the shirt, turning it over in his hands as if searching for something hidden. Then, slowly, he lifts it to his face and sniffs it. He stands still for a moment, as if thinking—then, without warning, he rips it apart.

One strip at a time.

The sound of tearing fabric fills the room, each rip slow and deliberate. His movements are steady, controlled. It doesn't feel like an act of rebellion. It feels... ritualistic.

I stare at him, frozen. Should I be angry? Amused?

A ridiculous thought crosses my mind—maybe he has his own sense of style. Maybe my golem is a fashion critic.

I should laugh at the absurdity of it.

But instead, a strange excitement rises in me.

He didn't listen to me. And that gives me the perfect reason to buy him a shirt myself.

For the first time in my life, I will walk into a men's clothing store and choose something for someone who belongs to me.

I picture it so clearly—walking into the store, standing tall, telling the saleswoman, "I need a shirt for a broad-shouldered man." I imagine the flicker of envy in her eyes as she wonders about the man I'm shopping for.

This simple act—so normal, so routine—will make Saul real in a way that nothing else has.

The thought fills me with purpose.

The shop will be bright, filled with busy saleswomen clicking their heels against the polished floor. They will flutter around, calling to each other in sharp voices, their arms draped with clothes.

I know exactly the kind of woman they are. I have feared them my whole life.

They move in packs, circling thin, elegant customers, their voices dripping with praise—"It's perfect!" Their confidence is unshakable, their opinions absolute.

To them, I have always been nothing. Either invisible or embarrassingly obvious.

They have a way of looking at you, slicing through you with a single glance—sizing up your hips, your outfit, your worth. Their dismissive looks have pushed me out of stores so many times, but not before I grabbed something—anything—just to avoid the shame of walking out empty-handed.

I've left stores clutching skirts that didn't fit, shirts that clung in all the wrong places, clothes that would sit in the back of my closet, untouched. I never wanted their approval, but I always felt their judgment.

I remember the worst of it—the way they smirked as I bought a hideous brocade skirt, their contempt following me out the door.

But this time, I won't be shopping for myself.

This time, I will belong in that store. Because this time, I am buying something for him.

But today is different. Not this time.

My heels tap confidently—click-clack, click-clack—as I walk across the store, feeling like I belong. One of the saleswomen notices me from a distance, her sharp eyes scanning me, sizing me up as she strides over, confident like a hunter moving in on its prey.

"Excuse me," I say, lifting my chin just a little. "I'm looking for a men's shirt." My voice is steady, my expression calm. It works—her gaze softens, losing its edge.

"He's tall, broad-shouldered, dark-skinned," I continue, letting each word land with weight. I watch as her posture changes, the authority fading from her stance. By the time I finish speaking, she no longer looks like an intimidating saleswoman—just another person, one who probably curls up alone at night, just like the rest of us.

"I'll bring some shirts right away," she says, her tone almost respectful now. "Does he—or you—have a color preference?"

"There's only one choice," I say with a small smile. "Navy blue."

She hurries off and returns with a few options, but none of them feel right. "Would you like me to bring more?" she asks, eager to please. I nod, watching her rush back and forth until finally, she brings the perfect one. Large, rich, a deep blue that matches exactly what I had in mind. Satisfaction settles over me.

For the first time, I feel like someone. Like a woman choosing clothes for her man.

Confidence surges through me. "Actually," I say, as if the thought just came to me, "I'd like to try something on for myself." Not this time, little shopgirl—no more awful skirts that don't fit.

I leave the store triumphant, my arms full of shopping bags. I take the stairs two at a time, each step feeling like a small victory—over loneliness, over doubt, over the parts of myself I've spent years trying to hide. I can't wait to see him wear it, to see how my choice fits him.

Outside a nearby apartment, a small boy sits on the doorstep, his head resting in his hands, staring at the ground. It's one of Haya's kids, usually nosy and full of questions. But today, he doesn't look at me. His whole posture seems weighed down by something heavy.

"Congratulations," I say gently, but he doesn't lift his head.

"What did your mom have?" I ask, my voice soft, playful. I know it's the wrong approach—kids are smarter than we give them credit for, and pretending doesn't fool them. But I can't help myself. "A boy or a girl?"

"Boys," he mutters, eyes fixed on a tiny gecko trapped in the corner.

"Twins?" I exclaim, forcing some enthusiasm. "That's amazing!"

I lean in, meaning to give him a quick hug, but he pulls away like I might burn him.

"What are their names?" I ask, then immediately regret it. "Oh, never mind—you'll tell us at the bris, right?"

"No," he mumbles, barely above a whisper. "There won't be a bris."

I try to guess. "Oh, because they're too small?"

"No!" His voice cracks, and something in him seems to break. "Because they're attached!"

Then he bolts, shouting over his shoulder, "Ugly freaks!"

The shopping bags slip from my hands.

When I walk into the apartment, Saul is standing there, buttoning up the shirt I bought for him.

It fits perfectly.

The deep blue fabric clings to his body, showing every sharp angle, every strong line. The color matches the veins under his skin, and I can't stop staring. He looks whole. Flawless. Perfect.

Unlike—

I push the thought away.

"Wait," I say, stepping toward him. "Let me do it."

I finish buttoning the shirt, smoothing the fabric into place, tucking it into his dark trousers. The act feels strangely tender—like dressing a child. But at the same time, there's something else, something electric that makes every nerve in my body feel too aware, too alive.

That feeling returns—that awful, sticky sensation, like a slow-moving snail dragging itself down my thigh, leaving behind something slick and humiliating. My body is leaking want, and I press my legs together, trying to make it stop.

Saul watches me the whole time.

A slow, knowing smirk plays on his lips.

It's mocking. Teasing. Like he's daring me to say it out loud. Go ahead. Ask me. Tell me what you want.

But he knows I won't. He knows I can't.

Because asking would mean exposing everything—admitting the need, the hunger, the shame of wanting him this much.

I can't do it.

Because if I ask, there's a chance he'll say no. And if he does, that would prove what I've feared all along—that I am unworthy. That I am unlovable.

Saul seems to understand this. He waits, his silence thick with power.

And I hate him for it.

Bastard.

The knock on the door makes me jump.

It's loud, firm, impatient. Let me in. Let me in.

I already know who it is.

Since the day I moved in, this door has been nothing but a portal for unwanted guests—people who bring nothing but stress, criticism, and unwanted advice.

My stomach twists. But I force it down. Calm down, Telma. Act normal.

I open the door, trying to keep my face neutral.

But inside, I'm already seething.

They sweep inside—my parents.

Or, as I call them in my head: Gila and Reuven. The original architects of my self-doubt. My natural-born enemies.

My father sniffs the air, already looking for something to disapprove of. My mother clutches a plastic shopping bag, something bulky and woolen inside.

I can already tell what it is.

A hideous, oversized sweatsuit.

I swallow back the urge to snap, I sleep naked, Mother. What exactly do you think I need that for?

"What a surprise," I say, quickly grabbing newspapers and scattered photos from the couch. With a nudge of my foot, I slide a few candy wrappers under the armchair, suddenly hyper-aware of the mess everywhere. The clutter, the dust—how did I not notice it before?

"Why didn't you let me know you were coming?" I add, keeping my voice light, aiming for the polite surprise of a host caught off guard.

Reuven narrows his eyes. He doesn't buy it. He moves through the room like some oversized rodent, pausing to inspect a needlepoint tapestry I turned to face the wall.

"But Telma," my mother says, her voice carrying just the right amount of exasperation to irritate me, "I told you we were coming a few days after Seder to collect Grandma's holy books for the synagogue donation. I even mentioned it at the table."

Of course, I don't remember this at all. The Seder was a blur—too much noise, too much wine. When exactly was she supposed to have said this? While Moses glared at me from the Haggadah illustrations? While I was drinking Elijah's wine? I picture that accusing face now, sneering, Daughter of Egypt! Little Pharaoh!

Maybe they made the whole thing up, knowing I'd been too out of it to object.

They settle in like they own the place, reclaiming lost territory. My father leans back, slurping his lukewarm tea, each noisy sip clawing at my nerves. I clench my fists and think, Choke on it, Reuven. Just choke.

My mother hovers awkwardly, unsure where to place the bag holding that awful sweatsuit. Her eyes sweep across the room, taking in every inch of dust, every faded photograph, every crooked stack of books. I can feel her judgment without her saying a word. She catalogues every failure, every sign of neglect. Then, finally, she looks at me. I feel that gaze like a weight pressing down on my chest.

And just like that, they pull me into their world.

It's not what they say. It's not even what they do. It's them. Their presence, their endless cycle of disappointment and small, tired dreams.

My father, always talking about the Warsaw house we'll never see again. My mother, always listing her aches and pains. And me—their daughter—slowly becoming them, trapped in the same pattern, tethered to their life by something invisible but unbreakable.

I see it so clearly: the sighing, the slurping, the endless complaints. And worst of all, the creeping realization that I'm becoming like them.

The thought makes my stomach turn.

Tears push at the edges of my eyes, frustration rising in my throat. But something stops them, holds them back. The usual flood of emotions doesn't come. Instead, there's something else—something grounding me, keeping me steady.

Wait. There's something more important right now.

And there is.

The attic feels warmer than usual, like it's holding its breath. Saul stands there, still as a statue, his dark blue shirt making him look almost festive.

But he's calm. Completely calm.

And that calm reaches me, cooling the fire inside, yet at the same time, making something else stir. Something sharp and alive.

"My parents are downstairs," I whisper, as if saying it too loudly might summon them.

His expression shifts—just slightly. A flicker of something in his dark eyes, something almost amused.

That tiny smirk infuriates me.

As if he's enjoying this. As if watching me squirm is entertainment.

"Please, try not to make any noise," I say, stepping closer.

The space between us thickens.

I can feel my body waking up under his gaze, like every inch of skin has suddenly become aware of itself. The air crackles between us, full of heat and something dangerous, something unspoken.

It's not just want. It's need.

And for once, it doesn't make me feel weak. It makes me feel alive.

Downstairs, my parents sit like ghosts, sipping their weak tea, clinging to their dull, gray existence. Their world is stale, filled with regrets and empty routines.

And I want Saul to pull me away from it.

To burn me up.

To take me into something real.

But I can't say it.

Ask him. Tell him. Command him. Beg him.

No.

The words lodge in my throat, heavy and stuck. Why do things always have to be said out loud? Why do words always betray me?

My whole life has been a series of almosts. Almost saying the right thing. Almost choosing the right path. Always walking next to happiness, but never stepping into it.

And now, I stand beside him, close enough to feel the heat of his skin, and I still can't say the words.

He watches me with maddening patience, as if to say, Sorry, but I can't read minds, Madame.

Downstairs, silence lingers in the air, thick with unspoken words.

I feel it before I even enter the room.

My parents glance at me with that mix of concern and irritation they've perfected over the years. I don't react. Instead, I open a packet of stale crackers, breaking them in my hands. They taste like dust and soap, but I chew them anyway, letting the crunch fill the emptiness.

The boxes slowly fill with books—Grandma's old religious texts, packed up for donation.

But I don't care. The only book that matters is hidden far beyond their reach.

My father rifles through the shelves, his nosy energy as strong as ever. My mother stands beside him, blinking rapidly, her face caught between disapproval and exhaustion. She looks like an old owl, her head twitching as she scans the spines of the books.

Behind her, the needlepoint fawn on the wall smiles its eternal, empty smile.

"So, Simon's off to Poland, huh?" my father says suddenly, holding up a worn book like some grand discovery. His tone is sharp, pointed, filled with something smug.

The meaning is clear.

So, you couldn't keep him, could you?

窗体顶端

窗体底端

I stay silent, my eyes locked on the book in his hands. I shouldn't have left it there. What other mistakes have I made?

"I gave him a small job," Father says, clearly enjoying this topic. "There's a man in Warsaw who says he has documents proving the house belonged to us. A respectable Jewish family. None of this hero nonsense." He shoots a sharp look at Mother.

And just like that, the argument begins. The same one they've had for years. They know their lines by heart, their voices rising and falling in a familiar rhythm.

Mother snaps back, her tone cold. "You only say that because your family's house is still full of Poles! You can't give my mother credit for getting hers back."

I don't need to listen to know what comes next. Their fights are as predictable as the tide. Accusations thrown back and forth, like a routine they refuse to break.

"Oh sure, big-time rebels!" Father scoffs, clearing his throat like he's about to land the final blow.

Mother waves him off, her expression tight. They're stuck in this endless cycle, locked in a battle neither of them will ever win. Maybe they don't even want to. Maybe this fight is all they have left holding them together.

Then—THUD. A sudden, loud noise from the attic.

They freeze, both heads snapping toward the ceiling.

"What was that?" Father's voice is sharp with suspicion.

Panic rises in my throat, and I blurt out, "Oh, that? Just... uh... the Passover dishes. Nili's stuff. I haven't sorted them yet, and

186

everything's stacked too high. Super unstable. Last night two big pots fell, scared me half to death, blah blah blah…"

I stop too late. Their eyes narrow at the same time. Suspicion replaces curiosity. Why didn't I just brush it off? Why didn't I just say, None of your business, you nosy jerks?

I race upstairs, skipping steps, my heart pounding. I burst into the attic, and there's Saul, leaning against the wall like he belongs here. Like this is his home.

"What are you doing?" I hiss, my voice sharp and panicked. "Already planning to meet the family?" My sarcasm lingers in the air between us. Can a golem even understand irony? I don't care to find out.

My voice turns serious, cutting through my panic. "You will not move until they leave." The words leave my mouth like a blade, sharp and absolute.

Before my eyes, Saul changes. His strong, vibrant body seems to deflate. His muscles go slack, his posture limp like a puppet with cut strings. But his eyes—still burning, still full of life—lock onto me in silent protest. He has to obey. But I can feel his resistance in that stare.

This is it—my first real command. So why does it feel so wrong? Why is the first thing I do take away the very life I want from him? The thought twists inside me. My face burns with shame. I can't look at him anymore. I pull away, even though I'm standing right in front of him.

"I'll be right down!" I call over my shoulder, my voice shaky. I flee, but something inside me cracks open, spilling through me like fire. I press my legs together, trying to hold it in.

Downstairs, Gila and Reuven stand by the door. Their job is done.

Boxes packed, shelves emptied, their duty as parents performed with cold precision. Their concern is just an act, lingering in the air like cheap perfume.

I walk them to the door, desperate for them to leave so I can run back to the attic. Back to Saul. Back to whatever is happening inside me.

Father pauses, his small eyes narrowing as he stares at me. He smells the change in me, the secrets I carry.

Without warning, his hand shoots out, gripping my arm tightly.

"I see," he whispers, his face too close. "Don't think for a second that I don't see."

Our eyes lock. His cold blue against my gray. Father against daughter. Years of anger, blame, and something deeper—something neither of us will say out loud—pass between us.

I yank my arm free like his touch burns me. "Don't you dare touch me, you piece of shit," I spit, my voice shaking with fury. "You—"

Before I can finish, his hand swings up and smacks across my face.

The impact is like a gunshot. My head snaps back, slamming into the fuse box. Stars burst behind my eyes. My skin burns. My ears ring.

I stand there, stunned.

I have been slapped.

This man, this father of nothing, just hit me.

"Reuven!" Mother gasps, shocked, but she doesn't move.

A deep, burning rage rises inside me, wild and unstoppable. I see flashes in my mind—Father lying crumpled under the fuse box, his neck bent at a terrible angle, his empty eyes staring at nothing. Blood.

Pain. Death. Mother sobbing over his body. Me standing at his grave, feeling nothing. My fists tighten, and suddenly, I understand—I could do it. My hands, so small just moments ago, could destroy him.

I take a step forward, shaking with fury. He steps back, his face going pale, then turns and runs down the stairs. Mother follows, slower, her eyes filled with confusion and fear. Neither of them looks back. That's for the best. They wouldn't recognize me now—their little girl with a red cheek and wild eyes.

The insult stings as I rush up the stairs again, my feet moving faster than my thoughts. My face throbs where he struck me, my teeth clenched so hard I can feel the pain in my gums. My whole body feels like it's being torn apart, something inside me scratching to get out. My hands ache, my knuckles white.

Saul is waiting, his steady brown eyes watching me. He reaches out and presses his warm palm against my burning cheek. The touch is gentle, grounding me, pulling me back from the edge. I lean into him, the fire inside me cooling into something softer. His touch soothes me, but it can't take away what just happened.

I take his hand, leading him downstairs, moving forward with a certainty I don't fully understand. We head toward Grandma Gerta's room, a place heavy with fate, as if this moment was always meant to happen—long before I ever shaped him from the earth.

Something inside me has answered a call.

That truth settles over me, clear and sharp, separate from my tangled desires. I let him wrap me in his arms. I let him claim me. I am ready for this war, this battle that will define me. Everything that broke me led me here. And everything that prepared me has destroyed the rest.

Maybe love has nothing to do with it at all.

Around the bed, small figures appear, little versions of Telma, holding hands. Their laughter is light but eerie. They sway in a circle, singing in soft, haunting voices:

From earth and blood you knead the dough
    Watch until it rises so
Bake it and it turns to man
    Man then bakes you back again.

Oh yes, he will bake me back again. He will shape me, press his hands into my skin, and shove me into an oven until I come out changed—just like him.

We are so close now that his stillness presses against me like a wall. I breathe out, but there's no breath coming back from him. No movement. Then, a realization strikes me with terrifying clarity—he won't do anything until I tell him to. My hunger, my trembling, my burning desire—it all means nothing to him.

I brush my fingers against his chest, but he doesn't react. My body is aching, desperate, but he stands there, waiting. You pathetic, powerless woman.

The room is stifling, thick with heat that clings to my skin, making me sweat. Drops of moisture slide down my temples, down my neck, slipping between my breasts, pooling between my thighs. The heat grows, pulsing through me like a wave, but even this fire isn't enough to force the words out of my mouth.

I can't ask.

To say it out loud would be to admit the truth—to expose my weakness, my need. The words I refuse to say trap my shame inside me. This is my sin, raw and unforgiving.

And this man, standing before me, is the proof of that sin. He watches me with knowing eyes, taunting me. Go on, his gaze seems to say. Ask for it. Show me who you really are, doll.

The shame burns deep. I swallow hard, my throat dry.

"Please," I whisper, my voice shaking.

Still, he does not move.

The heat from his body seems alive, wrapping around me, suffocating and electrifying at the same time. My fingertips graze his chest again, and this time, the touch feels like fire licking my skin. My whole body throbs, my need so sharp it feels like it might tear me apart.

"Please," I try again, voice barely above a breath.

"Please, kiss me..."

Slowly, he lowers his head. His lips hover near mine, unbearably close. I can see the slight curve of his mouth. And in that moment, I know—he is smiling. And that smile is anything but kind.

"On my lips," I whisper, my voice breaking. My legs tremble beneath me.

His lips brush the corner of my mouth, my chin, the crease below my nose—light, indifferent kisses that set my skin on fire. They are not the kisses I begged for, but they still burn me to my core. And with each teasing touch, my last shred of resistance shatters.

He has won.

"Do it to me," I plead, unable to name what I want. The words themselves are humiliating, an admission of defeat. "Do it." My voice is unsteady, thick with fear and shame. "Do it hard, do it with force."

He grips my shoulders and lifts me off the ground with ease, his expression unreadable. He moves mechanically, like a puppet. Our eyes

Translated by Tim Zengerink

meet, and for a moment, he hesitates, as if considering what my words really mean.

"Please, have mercy," I whisper, my voice raw. "Don't make me keep asking... I won't say anything more..."

And just like that, he gives in.

He surrenders to the force we all pretend we can control. That thing inside us we try to separate from, but never truly can. Something inside him breaks, and suddenly, he is alive.

His hands grip me hard, molding me, pressing me into something new. He crushes me against him, and I feel it—fire, earth, power. And I knew, even before I shaped him from the dirt, that this was inevitable.

Somewhere far away, I hear flames crackling. The sound of something breaking inside me.

This is the end.

This is the beginning.

When it's over, the sheets are covered in dirt. Clumps of soil fall from my body as I move. I still feel the sting of the slap from earlier, the echo of it lingering on my skin.

I deserve it.

I am no longer human. I am a mannequin now, too—a hollow figure, trapped in a body reshaped by fire and earth, remade in his image.

# Chapter 17

Love is reflection of the self.

Telma stares into Saul's deep, earth-colored eyes and sees herself reflected back. What does she find there? Admiration, yes. Curiosity, definitely. And hidden between those emotions, something that almost looks like joy.

She watches how he reacts to her—the way he lingers on her face, the way his body responds to her touch, the way his eyes follow her every move. In that moment, something clicks inside her. For the first time in her life, Telma loves Telma.

I lie on Grandma Gerta's big bed, Saul's dark head resting against my arm. A strange sense of calm washes over me, softening the sharp, restless parts of me. My fingers trace gentle lines over his face, pausing on each feature I once shaped with my own hands. He is so still, so peaceful, and I let myself believe that means he is content. But deep down, I wonder—could it be something else?

What is he thinking about as he lies beside me? How does his golem-mind understand what we do here, in this bed, in this room? When I look into his dark eyes and see my reflection, do I see the real me? Or just what I want to believe?

I almost ask him. Almost. The words sit on my tongue: What are you thinking? But I can't bring myself to say them.

I have never told him to love me. Even I know love isn't something you can force. But that doesn't stop me from wondering—what is love? Could a being made of earth and willpower even feel it? He is gentle when he touches me, careful, almost reverent. Is that real? Or is he simply acting as he was created to?

The thought strikes me like a slap. If his kindness is just instinct, if it's built into him instead of freely given, then I will rip the paper from his mouth and watch him crumble back into the dirt he came from. If he isn't choosing this, then it isn't real. And if it isn't real, then I have been fooling myself.

But isn't this what you wanted, Telma?

No. Not anymore.

Now, Telma wants something else.

She wonders if love can grow on its own, without commands or control. She imagines tiny flowers sprouting from his dark body, vines curling around his wrists, delicate petals blooming on his head. If only love worked that way—obvious, visible, undeniable. Humans don't have that luxury. They fill the air with sweet words, empty promises, clever lies. But Saul… Saul can't lie. Or can he?

I search his eyes for answers. Do they soften when he looks at me? Do they lighten, just a little, as if something deeper is rising to the surface? Or am I just seeing what I want to see?

But none of that matters right now. Because at this moment, I am happy.

The bed beneath us grows dirtier every day, but I don't care.

The missing stack of history exams spills from my teacher's bag as I adjust my hair in the mirror. I crouch to pick them up, unwilling to let those terrible wartime stories seep into this space, into this part of my life. My fingers slide through my dark hair—it feels fuller, healthier, more alive than ever before.

I glance at Saul, sitting quietly on the bed, waiting.

"How do I look?" My voice is lower, huskier now, roughened by the changes in me. This new voice forces me to choose my words carefully, giving everything I say an unintentional sharpness.

As always, Saul listens. His dark eyes lock onto mine, steady, unblinking. His gaze makes me blush—an unfamiliar feeling. He doesn't look at me like a creation looking at its maker. No, he looks at me like a man looking at a woman.

And how perfect it is.

There is no one else for him to compare me to, no impossible standards I must meet. To him, I am it. I am beauty itself, without flaw, without competition. My body, every soft or imperfect part, is enough. This is how things should be. Simple. Right.

I step toward him, hesitating only for a moment before pressing my hand to the lighter patch of skin on his chest. I sit beside him, and he buries his head in my chest, wrapping his arms around me. I close my eyes, letting myself melt into the moment, letting myself believe that this feeling will last forever.

"Saul," I murmur, "I'll be late for school."

Then I see it.

In the corner of the room, a tiny gecko twists in the shadows, its nearly see-through tails flickering in and out of the light. Saul tenses in my arms, and suddenly, the air in the room feels different. Something unspoken lingers between us.

Disgust twists in my stomach. My skin turns pale as I stare at the writhing little creature, its two tails twitching in a way that makes my whole body shudder. But Saul doesn't move. He just stands there, frozen, his deep brown eyes locked on the gecko with an intensity that unsettles me.

"Kill it!" I scream, my voice raw and cracking.

He hesitates.

Rage surges through me, and I shriek, my throat burning from the force of it. "Kill that thing!"

Slowly, as if reluctant, Saul steps toward the corner. He reaches down and grabs the gecko by one of its flailing tails. The creature thrashes in his grip as he closes his fingers around it. His movements are oddly gentle, but his eyes hold something deeper—something I can't quite understand. His hand tightens, and I know he's about to crush it.

"No!" The word bursts from me, panicked. "Don't move! Don't do it!"

Instantly, his body relaxes. He looks at me, confused, waiting for an answer. But I don't give one.

The gecko lives.

Without another word, I grab my teacher's bag and rush out of the room. I need to get away—from that awful, unnatural thing, from the chaos slithering into my home. I need order. I need normalcy. I need the clear, steady rhythm of a school bell marking the beginning and end of things.

But my legs take me somewhere else.

Sometimes, your body knows where you need to go before your mind does. My feet carry me, not toward school, but down the familiar streets that lead to my mother's house. The April sun beats down, and I try to dodge the burning light, longing for the cool shade inside her home.

She'll be happy to see me, I tell myself. Isn't that what mothers do? Feel joy when their daughters visit, even if that daughter is me?

"What a surprise!" she says as she opens the door.

She's wearing one of Father's old bathrobes, her small frame lost in the oversized fabric. I pause in the doorway, taking her in. This woman who carried me, who gave me life. I remember the night in the cemetery, the way the earth groaned and trembled as I shaped Saul, as if it, too, was in labor. I remember how my own body shook from the weight of creation. Bringing something into the world always takes something from you—something you never get back.

"Is everything okay?" I ask, forcing a smile. I want this visit to be different, to keep it from turning into another strained conversation.

"Uh… I don't know," she says, hesitating. Then, more firmly, "You look wonderful, Telma."

Telma, five years old.

She sits on the floor, her little braids sticking out, her big eyes filled with questions only children are brave enough to ask.

"Mommy," she says in her small, hopeful voice, "is Nili pretty?"

Mother's hands fumble with the jars on her dressing table. She rubs a sharp-smelling cream into her neck, her eyes fixed on anything but her daughter.

"Yes," she says at last, her voice flat. "Nili is very pretty."

Telma waits. She already knows how the story should go. Every fairy tale, every bedtime tale, ends the same way: But you are even prettier, my lovely daughter.

She waits as her mother massages the cream into her skin. Waits, because she still believes the words will come.

But they don't.

"And… what about me?" she finally asks, the pause stretching too long.

"You are, too," Mother says, and just like that, the words carve themselves into her heart, becoming a secret definition of ugly.

Now, standing here in her home, I feel something different. A warmth, unfamiliar but bright, starts to grow inside me. It blends with the spark Saul has awakened in me. For the first time, I think maybe—just maybe—I might be beautiful.

I smile at Mother, a real smile. But the moment fades as I take in the room around us.

It's a mess.

Dirty glasses pile up on the table, old newspapers litter the floor. A once-thriving plant in the corner has shriveled, its brown leaves scattered. The floor is sticky in places, and a crumpled wrapper peeks out from beneath the carpet.

"What happened to your voice?" Mother asks suddenly, her forehead creased with concern. She picks up a glass, her movements slow and careful, like someone who is afraid to break.

"It'll be fine," I say, trying to sound reassuring. "But you don't look well. Are you sick?"

"I don't know," she murmurs, avoiding my eyes. "What about you?"

Me?

What could I possibly say?

That my heart is bursting with something wild and new? That I have found love—strange, messy, impossible to ignore? That my bed is stained with earth, proof of the life I have created?

But I look at her, wrapped in that old bathrobe, her body small, her voice uncertain, and I say nothing.

We sit together in the dusty living room, sipping tea in silence. Her hands are delicate, her spoon clinking softly against the cup. The frailty in her movements unsettles me. I have always known my mother was fragile in spirit, but now, for the first time, I see that her body is fragile, too.

"Your father wanted to take me to the hospital," Mother says after a long pause.

"Why didn't you go?"

She doesn't answer. But we both know why. She has always avoided doctors, trusting them only when she had no other choice. The only time she let Father take her was when she gave birth to me. "You came out in under a minute!" she always brags. I never understood why I was in such a hurry.

I try to remember a time when my mother was sick, but nothing comes to mind. It was always me—sniffling, running fevers, catching every little illness. But now, here she is, looking so small and frail. She has always been delicate in spirit, but her body was strong. Not anymore. Her pale face looks tired, worn down.

And then I smell it.

Not the usual scent of dust and clutter, but something else. Something sickly sweet, thick and heavy in the air. It fills my nose, making my stomach turn.

"Where does it hurt?" I ask, my voice catching.

"Down here," she says, folding her arms over her stomach. "The pain is strong, but I'll be fine." She gives me a faint smile, like she's trying to reassure me. But it only makes me more uneasy. The smell lingers, curling around me like something alive. My stomach churns. I swallow hard to keep from gagging.

"Look what Tzilla brought me yesterday," she says suddenly, pointing to a ceramic vase on the table. It's white and shiny, covered in red peach hearts. Their shape reminds me too much of raw, sliced meat. She beams with pride. "Isn't it beautiful?"

I barely glance at it. The overwhelming smell is pressing in on me, making it hard to focus.

"Mother," I say, forcing my voice to stay calm, "I think you're really sick. Very, very sick."

She waves a hand dismissively. "Oh, nonsense. You got better, didn't you? And look at you now. You're so pretty."

She laughs—a light, girlish sound. "Maybe when I get better, I'll look as good as you."

Two compliments in one hour. My whole life, I've waited for even one. And now, they spill from her so casually.

Warmth spreads through me, filling me with something strange and powerful. For the first time, I feel like I could do anything—set fire to the world and build it better than before. There is nothing Telma cannot do.

Mother watches me, studying my face, her hand resting absently on her stomach.

"Do you have a boyfriend, Telma dear?" she asks, her voice playful.

My eyes flick to the door of my old bedroom. It hasn't changed. The same faded floral bedsheet, the same thin mattress, untouched for years. Even now, it holds the quiet loneliness of my childhood.

"Why do you ask?" I say carefully.

"Because you seem different," she says, narrowing her eyes slightly. "And you're acting differently."

"Different how?" I ask, curiosity creeping in. It's always unsettling to hear how others see you—to realize the version of yourself in their minds might not match the one in yours. But I still want to know.

"I don't know," she says, her gaze drifting. "You just suddenly seem so concerned about me. And earlier, when my stomach hurt really bad and I kind of convulsed, I noticed something… You flinched. Like you felt it, too."

Her words hit harder than I expect, sending a sharp twist through my chest.

"I remember how I felt when I fell in love with your father," she says, her voice softening with nostalgia. A dreamy, almost foolish look crosses her face, and I have to fight the urge to roll my eyes.

"I just wanted to do nice things for everyone," she goes on. "I even helped old ladies cross the street, whether they wanted to or not." She laughs lightly, lost in the past. I wish she'd stop. Something about seeing love on her face feels... wrong.

"And now here you are," she says, her voice warm. "Being so nice to me today. I thought maybe you were in love, too."

Her face suddenly flushes, as if every tiny vein beneath her skin has burst at once. And just like that, my own cheeks burn in response. My throat tightens.

Is this what she considers kindness? A short visit, a lukewarm cup of tea, a few half-hearted questions about her health?

Why does she settle for so little?

She finishes the last drops of her tea and gives me a small, grateful smile. I can't bring myself to return it.

I look away, my hands twisting in my lap.

Yes, Mother. I am being nice to you.

Nice at your expense.

# Chapter 26

Your bed feels enormous. You lie in the middle of it, small and alone, like a single pea lost in a sea of white sheets. Your mind drifts, empty, unable to focus on the one thought that has haunted you since you walked through the door. From the moment you scrubbed the soot from your skin to the second you collapsed into the pillows, the question has lingered, unspoken but heavy:

Will you ever see him again?

Could it be that he's hurt, burned, turned to ash like the little dolls swallowed by fire? The thought lands with a dull thud: today is Lag B'Omer, the holiday of flames. Maybe the fire has taken another sacrifice—another creation of yours, lost to the heat.

No. That can't be. He isn't gone. You are the only one who can destroy him, and you haven't. Not yet. Not now. Not now.

But the fear doesn't leave you. You want him here, beside you, his familiar warmth filling the empty space in your bed. You want him. And yet… what if he never comes back?

Never comes back.

The words settle in your mind like cold, hard stone. He's not coming back. Ever. How foolish you were to believe otherwise.

You start to doubt yourself. Did you really see him at school, or was it just a trick of your imagination, something your heart made up? If he was there, why didn't he come home with you? Where is he now?

Your thoughts race, running in circles. What is he doing out there, this creature of earth and fire? What is he seeing? What is he thinking? But you're not afraid for him. You know he can survive. Life with you, Telma, has surely prepared him for anything.

So why hasn't he come back?

Has he figured you out? Seen the worst parts of you—the selfishness, the neediness, the fears you try to hide? Maybe he finally understands just how much you rely on him, how dependent you are. The same insecure thoughts that haunt women when their men leave creep into your mind. You can almost hear him saying it: It's not you, it's me.

The irony doesn't escape you.

Your sleep is restless. You toss and turn in the empty bed, your body searching for the weight of someone beside you. How strange that you got used to his presence so fast. And now, as the hours drag on, the truth settles in: you will sleep alone again. Just as you always have. Just as you always will.

Then—

A sound.

You jolt awake.

What was that?

The house feels different, as if it's floating, untethered. Outside, the silver moon stares through the window. It always seems full when you are uneasy, its pale light cold and judging. You remember how it glowed at Grandma Gerta's funeral, watching as if it knew every secret. It was full the night you created Saul, too, a silent witness to everything.

And now? Now it hangs slightly deflated, like something unfinished. How you hate that glowing orb. Isn't there a story that says the moon was once part of the Earth before breaking away? Like all things that leave, it never really disappears. It just circles endlessly, watching.

Then—

A noise. Slow, heavy footsteps dragging across the floor.

Your heart leaps.

Could it be?

Is he back?

A thousand thoughts crash together, making you dizzy. What will you say? How will you welcome him?

Your body betrays you. You squeeze your eyes shut, pretending to sleep. Really, Telma? This is what you've stooped to? Childish games? Yet you can't move, can't bring yourself to make things easy for him. Somewhere deep inside, that insecure part of you demands that he prove himself.

Then—

Warmth.

Before you see him, you feel him. The heat of his body presses against the air, heavy and inescapable. He stands over you, silent. You shrink under the weight of his presence. He is watching you, studying you.

Does he still think you're beautiful? Did he ever?

Your mind spirals. Has he seen other women while he was gone? Soft lips, warm skin, curves that aren't yours? What if, now that he's back, he's comparing you to what he's seen?

The panic takes hold, and your eyes snap open.

He is there.

Towering over you, unmoving. His eyes locked on yours.

You force a small, hesitant smile.

Nothing.

He doesn't react. His face is still, unreadable.

You try again, widening your smile, stretching it so far it almost hurts. You bare your gums in desperation, hoping to break through his silence.

Still, nothing.

Something cold trickles through you. A flicker of doubt.

Why does he feel different? Have you done something wrong?

Then—

Without warning, he moves.

His hands reach for you, lifting you effortlessly into his arms. He carries you like you weigh nothing. His strength should be comforting, but instead—

The smell of smoke lingers on him.

It coils around you, seeping into your thoughts. You should feel relieved, but his touch is stiff, distant. He holds you like an object, not a person.

You don't cry, though maybe you should. His grip isn't gentle. He doesn't cradle you the way you imagined. He carries you with purpose, detached, as if you are nothing but dust in his hands.

The moonlight slices through the room like a blade, sharp and bright.

To your left, a tiny sound—

A laugh.

Your eyes dart to the source.

The needlepoint fawn.

Its stitched mouth twisted in a mocking grin.

You swallow hard, forcing yourself to breathe.

Imagine, you tell yourself.

Imagine you are a bride, carried by her husband. Imagine he holds you close because he wants to, because you are his and he is yours.

Ignore the doubt creeping in.

Isn't this what you always wanted?

Saul is yours now. Forever.

All you have to do is wait.

But Saul doesn't stop. He carries you up the narrow attic stairs, his steps steady, his movements stiff and unnatural. In the small, dusty space, he sets you down among old shelves and forgotten things, like a package dropped at its final destination.

Your bare feet land on broken glass—shattered jam jars. The sharp edges dig into your skin, and you feel warm blood mix with the sticky remains of peaches. The metallic scent of blood and the thick, sugary smell of fruit fill your nose. The room tilts, your tongue heavy in your mouth.

Then—

You jolt awake.

A sharp, jarring sound cuts through the silence. Your heart pounds. What is that? You strain to listen.

Fool.

It's the telephone.

You're still in bed, alone. Outside, the sky glows with the soft pinks and golds of dawn, the horizon brushed with the faded colors of an old painting.

And Saul—he isn't here.

You can't stay in bed another second. The sheets are cold. The floor is colder. The idea of answering the phone doesn't even cross your mind. Whoever it is, it can't be him.

You drift into Grandpa's office, your eyes landing on the old photographs.

There's your grandmother—her lips curved into a smile, her bright eyes filled with a joy that seems almost too much. Her frozen expression feels like a riddle, something hidden beneath the black-and-white surface.

What you wouldn't give to know when that picture was taken. Before or after she created the golem?

But does it matter?

The answer is already written all over your face, pressed into the empty bed you just left behind.

If Grandma Gerta were here, what would she say? You can almost hear the sharp, teasing words she'd throw at you, the knowing look in her eyes. You hate the scattered pieces of her that linger inside you, unfinished and unsatisfying. You want to erase that smug little smile from her picture—or maybe, just maybe, take it for yourself.

Because this is your story now, isn't it? Not hers.

Right?

But you never asked how her story ended, did you? You were too busy being a child, laughing at the edges of her tales, never realizing they held something more. And now, look at you. Alone. Wrapped in an old bathrobe, clutching faded photographs like some desperate fool.

And then—

A sound.

The slow, dragging weight of heavy footsteps.

You freeze.

The steps are steady, deliberate—undeniably his. They stop outside your door.

The air shifts.

The door bursts open. A rush of heat follows.

Saul.

For a moment, the world tilts. Your head swims. Is this real?

But yes—he is here. His presence pulls everything into focus, anchoring you. Those dark, knowing eyes have seen so much. And yet, they still found their way back to you.

You don't ask why. You don't question anything. You don't even notice the photographs slipping from your trembling hands.

You just run to him.

A wild, reckless joy surges through you, raw and overwhelming. It is the kind of joy that always comes before a great fall—but you don't care. His arms close around you, strong and sure. He holds you tightly, and in that embrace, there is only one truth: he came back.

This—this moment—is the greatest gift he has ever given you. Second only to the kiss you still dream of but have yet to receive.

Your face tilts upward. The space between you disappears. His breath is warm against your lips. You don't hesitate. You want him to take everything—every breath, every piece of you—into himself.

His hand moves, fingers brushing against your lips, tasting of earth, of life and death entwined. You close your eyes, surrendering.

The scent of smoke lingers between you. Heat flares against your skin, flames licking at the edges of the moment. Your hair stirs as if caught in an unseen wind, your body dusted with soot.

Your lips part, waiting—

Then—

The door slams open.

The force rattles the walls, sending flecks of plaster crumbling to the floor.

Simon stands in the doorway, his expression cold, his presence thick with something awful.

"I just came from the hospital," he says, voice flat.

A pause. A breath.

"Your mother is dead."

Two.

Your mind splits cleanly into two.

One part absorbs the words with a strange, empty calm.

Your mother is dead.

The finality of it is absolute.

Dead.

Mother.

Dead.

But what does that even mean? The weight of it doesn't fully sink in, clouded by your own confusion.

Yet, part of you is completely aware of what's happening right in front of you.

Simon and Saul are staring at each other for the first time.

Their eyes lock above your head, the air between them crackling with tension. The room feels like a storm about to break.

Simon's fingers twitch at his side.

Your mother is dead.

Saul doesn't flinch.

Dead.

His lips press into a firm line, his eyes narrowing in silent focus. Poor Mother—even in death, she cannot hold your full attention.

The standoff continues. A battle with no words, just two men locked in an invisible struggle. You stand in the middle, dazed, your mind unable to keep up with what's unfolding.

Then—

Simon moves.

In a sudden, shocking motion, he thrusts his hand into Saul's mouth.

His mouth.

The same mouth that was supposed to kiss you. The one you had dreamed about, waited for. The mouth that holds the slip of paper— the one thing keeping Saul alive.

A violent shudder runs through you. This is wrong. This is violence in its purest form.

"I told you," Simon snarls, his face red with anger. "If you can't do it, I will!"

His hand pushes deeper, his fingers grasping wildly.

Then—

A scream.

Raw. Animalistic. Terrifying.

Your hands fly to your own mouth, but the scream isn't yours.

It's Simon's.

Blood drips from his arm, thick and dark, pooling onto the floor.

Saul has bitten him.

You've never seen Saul's teeth before. Never knew how sharp they could be. But now, his mouth is open, and his teeth gleam in the dim light like the edge of a blade.

Still, Simon doesn't back down. Even through the pain, he lunges again, his uninjured hand reaching forward. "I'll kill you!" he shouts, voice wild with rage.

Saul doesn't hesitate. His hands clamp around Simon's throat, powerful and unyielding. He starts to squeeze.

But he doesn't take his eyes off you.

Even as Simon struggles, gasping for air, clawing at Saul's arms— Saul is watching you.

His hands tighten. Simon's face turns red, then purple. His breaths come in weak, choked gasps. Yet even in his final moments, he doesn't stop fighting. He grips Saul's lower lip and pulls, his fingers digging deep.

Somewhere, a clock chimes softly, out of place in the chaos.

You watch, frozen.

This feels familiar. Like something you've already imagined before. Like a memory, playing out in real time.

Two men, fighting to the death.

But neither one is looking at each other.

They are only looking at you.

Simon gurgles, his voice barely there. "Tell him... tell him to stop. He's killing me..."

The words hit like a strike to your chest.

You hesitate.

If you tell Saul to stop, Simon will live—and win.

You can already picture it. Simon's hand tearing the slip of paper from Saul's mouth. Saul's body breaking apart, crumbling into nothing but dirt and dust.

Gone.

You don't want that.

Simon's eyes roll back. His hands go limp. His tongue slips from his mouth, his skin going ghostly pale.

A spike of panic shoots through you.

Before you can stop yourself, the words spill out:

"Enough, Saul! Stop! Leave him be!"

The moment you say it, you know it's a mistake.

Saul flinches.

His whole body stiffens, his grip faltering just slightly. His eyes snap to yours, full of something unreadable. Hurt? Betrayal? Sadness?

You can't tell.

But Simon sees his chance.

With a desperate burst of energy, he lunges again. His hand shoots toward Saul's mouth—

Saul moves faster.

His hands tighten. His arms shift.

Then—

A sickening crack.

Simon's arm bends the wrong way. Bone snaps through skin, white against red.

Simon falls to the floor, screaming in agony. His body twists in pain, his broken arm hanging uselessly at his side. The air fills with the sound of his raw, jagged cries.

You shut your eyes, blocking it out.

When you open them, nothing has changed.

The two men remain where they are.

Saul, standing tall, silent, his expression unreadable.

Simon, crumpled on the floor, writhing in pain.

Their eyes are still locked, a battle that hasn't ended.

You can't take it anymore.

The weight of it all is crushing you, pulling at you from both sides, demanding something from you that you no longer have to give.

You turn and run. Let them destroy each other, let their anger consume them both. You don't care anymore. You just need to get away.

Your mother is dead.

The night air is hot and dry, stinging your tired eyes. You walk quickly, putting as much distance as possible between yourself and the suffocating weight of home. But as you move through the familiar streets—past the rustling orange trees, past the laughing children—you realize something.

The fight between Saul and Simon isn't just happening back in your apartment. It's inside you, too. It has always been there. And it will never truly end.

At the end of the street, a figure steps out from the shadows. The moonlight catches her hair, making it glow like a halo.

Nili.

"I heard about your mother," she says when you reach her. Her voice is quiet, almost gentle. "I'm so sorry."

You study her, surprised by the sudden connection you feel. For the first time, she doesn't seem like a rival, someone untouchable and distant. She is just Nili—human, flawed, as breakable as you.

Something unspoken passes between you. You both come from the same tangled roots, tied to the same complicated history. The same blood, the same strange pull that neither of you can explain.

"How did you find out?" Your voice sounds flat, distant.

"Simon told me," she says.

His name stirs nothing in you. No anger, no sadness. Just exhaustion.

"We were supposed to go to your place together," she adds.

But you barely hear her. Your mind is back in that apartment, trapped with the two men you left behind, locked in their endless fight.

"He's already there."

"Can I go now?" Your voice is hoarse, thin.

"No. Not yet."

She reaches for you suddenly, her fingers closing tightly around your elbow. Her grip is firm, almost desperate.

"Telma," she says, her voice shaking now. She squeezes your arm like she's afraid you'll disappear if she lets go. Her wide eyes hold something you don't expect—fear. Real, raw fear.

You don't ask what's wrong. You already know.

"Everything will be fine," you whisper, though you don't believe it. The words feel empty, lifeless. Your body feels unbearably heavy, your mind foggy with exhaustion. You want to collapse right here on the pavement, let the heat of the ground seep into you while Nili stands over you, guarding the world from pressing in.

"I'm going to my father's house," you say suddenly, the words surprising even you. You haven't thought about him once tonight. The guilt is sharp and sudden.

"I can come with you," Nili offers, uncertain. You can tell she doesn't want to be alone either.

"All right." Your voice is barely a whisper.

You walk together, two shadows stretching long behind you in the dim light. The wind tugs at the ribbons in your hair, playful, reminding you of something long past—two little girls, stepping carefully in their best white shoes, side by side, following a path they cannot change.

Your hearts beat in time, echoing a sorrowful, familiar rhythm:

Two gray eyes, two lips, a heart, a hollow place
Which is prettier? It doesn't matter anymore.

Your father's house is filled with darkness.

The air is thick, pressing down on you, smothering. You lift your eyes to the ceiling as if looking for an escape, but the windows are shut tight. Even the moon is locked out, its cold light denied entry. Maybe it isn't worthy of witnessing what's inside.

Maybe you aren't worthy either.

You don't want the moon's judgment, not tonight. You don't want it to see you lying beside Saul in silence. A silence so deep, so heavy, that it's worse than anger, worse than resentment. This silence is something else entirely. A void.

Saul's breath is steady beside you, deep and slow.

Your mother's breath has ended.

Her last moments, her final exhale, are part of the air now. They linger in this room, slipping into Saul's lungs, into yours, mixing, fading.

You wonder how many of her breaths touched his. How many still linger here, unseen, waiting.

Who will be next?

You see flashes of your father in your mind—his lost, broken expression as he wandered aimlessly through the house, hollow and empty. His wide, vacant eyes, his voice barely a whisper, saying her name just once before falling silent. Another person in your life whose lips have sealed shut, as if words no longer matter.

Deep inside, you know with absolute certainty that Saul is not evil. This isn't a guess—it's something you know. He could have hurt you countless times, could have destroyed the people around you, could have crushed Simon completely if he wanted to. But he didn't. He held back. Doesn't that mean something?

Then why, Telma, do you still feel this fear twisting inside you? Why does his presence feel like it carries something dark and dangerous?

Could it be that the real problem isn't Saul?

Could it be you?

Your own selfishness, your greed, your unwillingness to let go? Maybe it's time to stop looking outward for the cause and face the truth about yourself.

But you can't. You won't. You don't even want to try.

You lie beside Saul, the silence so heavy it feels like it's pressing down on your chest. Your whole life has been about avoiding things— avoiding choices, avoiding responsibility. You've always searched for the path of least resistance, the option that required no real decision.

But now, the moment of choice is coming. You can feel it closing in, suffocating.

Soon, you'll have to decide.

You'll have to face the truth about what you really want.

And yet—

You can't give him up.

No. No, no. The word pounds in your head, louder each time.

But how much longer can you defend him? How much longer can you stand by him while the people around you suffer? What if you are next?

Even if you wanted to end this, how could you? Saul has grown beyond you, become stronger than anything you could ever hope to control.

And yet...

You turn toward him in the darkness, searching his face for answers. Hoping for some kind of sign, a hint about what to do next. But he gives you nothing.

Just silence.

The doubt creeps in, slow and steady, like a shadow at the edge of your mind. How did he get so strong? And yet, why does he always come back? Was that his choice? Or was it because of you—because of the slip of paper hidden under his tongue, the words you placed there that night in the cemetery?

Did he return because he wanted to... or because you forced him to?

You shift closer, hesitating before leaning over him. His breath is warm against your skin, thick with the scent of damp earth and something faintly human. A shiver runs through you, a mix of familiarity and unease.

Slowly, you reach out, your fingers trembling as they brush against his face.

You trace the curve of his brow, smooth and unmarked. Your fingertips drift lower, brushing over his closed eyelids—so peaceful, so perfect, as if carved by a sculptor's hand. Then his nose, the shallow dip just below it, and finally—

His lips.

Warm. Familiar. But also foreign, unreadable.

Your fingers linger there, tracing their shape, feeling the strange contrast between softness and strength. His breathing deepens beneath your touch, but his body stays completely still. He doesn't move. He doesn't react.

And yet, your own breath hitches, uneven.

Why does this moment stir something inside you, Telma?

Could it be that you like this?

You let your fingertips glide over the smooth heat of his lips, marveling at the sensation—silk and fire. A flicker of boldness ignites inside you, and before you can stop yourself, the tip of your finger slips between them.

Slowly.

Carefully.

Inside, his lips are soft but strangely dry, lacking the warmth of a human mouth. The feeling is alien, unfamiliar. A strange thrill shoots through you, tangled with an unbearable tension. You are so close now, close to the very thing that makes him him.

But then—

Your fingertip meets resistance.

His teeth.

Sharp. Unmoving. A barrier, locked tight.

You hesitate.

Just a little farther…

You push gently, testing, pressing past—

A violent explosion of movement.

A force slams into you, hurling you backward like a rag doll.

You crash into the closet door with a sickening thud, your body crumbling to the floor.

Stars burst behind your eyes—green, purple, dazzling, blinding. Your head spins, the room tilting and twisting around you.

Pain crashes over you like a wave, sharp and merciless.

Your mouth fills with blood, hot and metallic, pooling on your tongue. Your nose feels like it's on fire, throbbing with a deep, unbearable ache. The entire left side of your face burns, pain radiating in waves.

It hurts.

It hurts so much.

And suddenly—

A memory surges forward.

You are ten years old again, small hands reaching for the cookie jar on the highest shelf.

The sweet smell of cookies fills the air, and you stretch higher, fingers just barely grazing the lid.

Then—

You slip.

You fall.

The jar crashes down with you, heavy glass colliding with your face.

The pain is instant.

The sharp, shattering crack of your nose breaking.

The sting of tears.

The sound of cookies scattering around you, a cruel, mocking rain.

And now, lying here, bleeding, hurting, you realize—

This is how it always is, Telma.

Everything you reach for.

Everything you want.

It always finds a way to break you.

# Chapter 30

Saul's lips press against mine, and suddenly, it's as if my entire body opens up at once. A flood of warmth, damp earth, and something deeper rushes over me. I hear voices in the distance, but their words blur into nothing. The world around me disappears, swallowed by this kiss—his kiss.

It takes over everything. I feel like I no longer exist as a person, only as a mouth. My tongue moves, brushing against my teeth, but I don't feel Saul's. Inside him, everything is soft, wet, endless. It's as if my tongue has slipped deep inside him, into a space I don't understand.

Where does all this moisture come from? What part of him holds so much of it?

The sound of collapsing buildings echoes in the distance. I taste something sweet—peaches, maybe. But I know it isn't real. None of it is. This moment, this kiss, is all that matters. This is what I have been waiting for. This is what a kiss should be.

And now, I have it.

I don't feel like myself anymore—I am part of him. I melt into him, into this kiss, into the gift he is giving me. He knows exactly what I need, always has. He must have realized that I could never bring myself to take the slip of paper from his mouth, never do what needed to be done.

So now, Saul is doing it for me.

I press closer, my heart pounding. Would I ever have been able to make this sacrifice on my own?

Saul, Saul, Saul. I love him.

Words swirl around us, unspoken but alive, fluttering like butterflies. Our lips stay locked, carrying a silent conversation no one else will ever understand. My whole body aches, tight with something I can't name, but suddenly, I see Saul more clearly than ever before.

Now, I understand.

I understand why I reached into the earth that night, why I created him, why he exists. And why I do, too.

Love.

Then—I feel it.

At the very edge of my tongue.

The slip of paper.

It lies there, soaked, hidden beneath Saul's tongue. My tongue brushes against it, and a shock runs through me. The texture is strange—elastic, alive. It tastes sharp, like metal, like blood. I can't move it. Every time I touch it, another jolt shoots through me, making me tremble.

I try to pull away, but Saul doesn't let me go. He holds me against him, his lips pressing harder, firmer.

And then—

Does he smile?

Is there the slightest curve to his lips?

Time stretches. I don't know if I am pulling the slip of paper toward me or if Saul is pushing it forward, but slowly—achingly slowly—it moves.

It slides between us, slipping past our lips, brushing against our teeth. It crosses from him to me, gliding into my mouth.

It settles beneath my tongue.

A perfect fit.

# Thank You for Reading

Dear Reader,

We hope this timeless classic has sparked your imagination and enriched your literary journey. Now that you've turned the final page, we want to share a vision for the future of reading—one where every classic you've ever wanted to explore is at your fingertips, in a format that best suits your life.

We'd like to invite you to gain immediate, unlimited digital & audiobook access to hundreds of the most treasured literary classics ever written—along with the option to secure deluxe paperback, hardcover & box set editions at printing cost. Together, we can spark a new global literary renaissance alongside our small, independent publishing house called "The Library of Alexandria."

Thousands of years ago, the Library of Alexandria stood as a beacon of knowledge—until it was lost to history. We aim to reignite that spirit of preservation and discovery right now, in the modern age—only this time, it's accessible to all, in every language and every format.

Picture a world where every timeless classic, novel, poem, or philosophical treatise is not only available to read but also updated for today's readers—modernized, translated into any language or dialect, and ready to enjoy in any format you choose, whether that is in an eBook, audiobook, paperback, or deluxe hardcover & box set version a printing cost.

By joining our movement to rebuild the modern Library of Alexandria, you become part of an unprecedented mission to offer:

- **Unlimited Audiobook & eBook Access to the Greatest Classics of All Time**

  Instantly explore thousands of legendary works, from Plato and Shakespeare to Jane Austen and Leo Tolstoy. All are instantly ready to read or listen to, giving you a complete literary universe at your fingertips.

- **Paperback & Deluxe Editions at Printing Costs:**

  Purchase any title in a paperback, deluxe hardbound, or deluxe boxset edition at printing costs, shipped right to your doorstep. Curate your personal library of Alexandria with editions worthy of display—crafted to last, designed to captivate, and delivered straight to your door.

- **Modern translations for Contemporary Readers in all languages and dialects**

  Discover a vast selection of classics reimagined in clear, current language—no more struggling with outdated phrases or obscure references. Next to the original versions, we aim to offer translations in as many languages and dialects as possible.

  As we continue our translation efforts and add new languages, readers everywhere can connect with these works as if they were written today. By bridging linguistic divides, you're contributing to ensuring that these timeless stories become more meaningful, accessible, and inspiring for people across the globe.

- **Your Personal Library of Alexandria:**

  Over the months and years, you'll curate a unique physical archive of classics—each volume a testament to your taste, curiosity, and love of knowledge. It's not just about owning books—it's about curating a cultural legacy you'll cherish and pass down for generations to come.

- **Join a Global Literary Renaissance:**

  Your support fuels an ongoing mission: allowing us to reinvest in offering deluxe print editions (including special boxsets) at their true cost, broaden the range of available formats and translations, and extend the reach of these works to new audiences worldwide. By joining today, you're not just preserving a legacy of masterpieces; you set in motion a powerful wave of literary accessibility.

  We are more than a publisher—we're a movement, and we can't do it alone. Your support lets us scale our mission, preserving and reimagining history's greatest works for tomorrow's readers.

**Become a Torchbearer of knowledge.**

Thank you for picking up this book and allowing us into your literary journey. As you turn the pages, know that you're part of something larger: a global effort to keep these stories alive, share their wisdom across borders and generations, and spark a true cultural revival for the modern era.

If this resonates with you—please consider taking the next step by visiting:

**www.libraryofalexandria.com**

With gratitude and a shared love of knowledge,

The Modern Library of Alexandria Team

Visit:

www.libraryofalexandria.com

Or scan the code below:

9 781804 217184